Plants & Gardens

Brooklyn Botanic Garden Record

WATER GARDENING

First Printing 1983
Revised Edition 1990
Second Printing, Revised Edition 1995

Brooklyn Botanic Garden

STAFF FOR THE ORIGINAL EDITION:

WILFRED V. SCHMIDLIN, GUEST EDITOR

BARBARA B. PESCH, EDITOR

MARGARET E.B. JOYNER, ASSOCIATE EDITOR

STAFF FOR THE REVISED EDITION:

BARBARA B. PESCH, DIRECTOR OF PUBLICATIONS

JANET MARINELLI, ASSOCIATE EDITOR

AND THE EDITORIAL COMMITTEE OF THE BROOKLYN BOTANIC GARDEN

ELENA BURINSKAS, ART DIRECTOR

JUDITH D. ZUK, PRESIDENT, BROOKLYN BOTANIC GARDEN

ELIZABETH SCHOLTZ, DIRECTOR EMERITUS, BROOKLYN BOTANIC GARDEN

STEPHEN K-M. TIM, VICE PRESIDENT, SCIENCE & PUBLICATIONS

Cover photograph by Christine M. Douglas

Plants and Gardens, Brooklyn Botanic Garden Record (ISSN 0362-5850) is published quarterly at 1000 Washington Ave., Brooklyn, N.Y. 11225, by the *Brooklyn Botanic Garden, Inc.* Second-class-postage paid at Brooklyn, N.Y., and at additional mailing offices. Subscriptions included in Botanic Garden membership dues ($25.00 per year), which includes newsletters, and announcements.

POSTMASTER: Send address changes to BROOKLYN BOTANIC GARDEN, Brooklyn, N.Y. 11225

ISBN #0-945352-14-X

PLANTS & GARDENS

BROOKLYN BOTANIC GARDEN RECORD

WATER GARDENING

Revised Edition of Vol. 41   No. 1   Handbook #106

■

CONTENTS

A garden pool containing water lilies.

FOREWORD

"A lake is the landscape's most beautiful and expressive feature. It is the earth's eye."

—Henry David Thoreau

Whether you agree with Thoreau that a water feature is the "earth's eye," it is a fact that the presence of water in the garden attracts the eye and soothes the spirit. Its sight and sound provide refreshment. Its most elegant expression is the water-lily pool.

Fossil evidence suggests that the Water Lily Family is old and evolutionarily primitive. Many of these plants remain in much the same form as 160 million years ago, an indication of their survival success.

The art of water gardening has been practiced for almost 3,500 years. Archaeological evidence indicates that irrigation ditches along the Nile were planted with water lilies and other aquatic plants. Members of this family also figure prominently in religious symbolism. Ancient Egyptians buried people of means with wreaths made of petals of water lilies. Lotus were found in the funeral wreaths of Ramses II.

Different cultures embellished or simplified pools. The Persians and Muslims created pools in elegant and formal designs. The Japanese turned to asymmetric shapes and replications of nature. Interest in water gardening accelerated in the Western world, especially in England, in the mid 1800s with the discovery in the tropics of *Victoria regia* (now *V. amazonica*).

Hybridizing of water lilies began in the late 1800s when Joseph Bory Latour-Marliac embarked on a breeding program and developed seventy varieties. Many Marliac varieties still remain in the trade.

Anyone who is interested can have a water garden. If you are fortunate enough to have a pond or the space to make one, the horizon is without limit. With less space, a small pool can be constructed and even an apartment terrace can house a small water lily in a tub.

Whether your water garden is a pond, pool, or bucket—enjoy it.

BARBARA B. PESCH
EDITOR

THE WATER GARDEN

WILLIAM TRICKER

Water Lilies, or Pond Lilies, have existed through the ages. The native [American] species, *Nymphaea odorata,* the white fragrant Pond Lily, was introduced into England in 1786. The English species, *Nymphaea alba,* also white, was recognized long before; these two species have become widely known and the general impression has been that all Water Lilies were white, hence the expression of surprise when one sees a red, yellow, or blue Lily for the first time.

Aquatics are associated with the ancient Egyptians in their literature. Mention is made of the Lotus or Water Lily, the name being applied both to Nelumbos [true lotus] and Nymphaeas [water lily], and, in fact, to several other plants in different parts of the Old World. Three distinct species are represented on many Egyptian monuments and are known to botanists and gardeners of the present day as *Nelumbo nucifera, Nymphaea lotus,* and *N. caerulea.* Nelumbiums were not only known to the Egyptians, but were common in the East and West Indies, China and Japan, Persia, and Asiatic Russia. The United States can also lay claim to one Lotus—*Nelumbo lutea*—the well-known yellow American Lotus.

WILFRED V. SCHMIDLIN, *President, William Tricker, Inc., Saddle River, N.J. Supplier of tropical water lilies to BBG for over 20 years. Guest editor of this Handbook.*

Amongst the many plants now grown for the embellishment of our gardens, public parks, and cemeteries, are hardy herbaceous plants, bulbs, annuals, tender plants known as bedding plants, sub-tropical plants, and last, but not least, aquatic plants. As Orchids are amongst greenhouse plants, so are aquatics amongst garden flowers, "The Elite." These are comparatively new and of recent introduction, though they have been known to collectors and a few cultivators for a number of years; but adaptability of them (including the most tender Nymphaeas and *Victoria regia*) for general culture out-of-doors in summer is a realization of recent date.

No class of plants is more widely distributed than Water Lilies, being indigenous to the United States, Canada, Central and South America, East and West Indies, Japan, China, Siberia, England, Europe, Austria, Africa, and Australia, each country possessing its own or several species of marked distinction, size and color. No class of plants possesses such diversity of color, including red, white, yellow, and blue, and intermediate shades. The members are no less distinctive in point of fragrance, as nearly all are possessed of an aromatic, delicate, and pleasing odor. They are also very unlike the host of other favorite flowers: some are day-blooming and close at night, others are night-blooming and close in the day. As a rule, the flowers open and close for three days or nights in succession, generally the first day flower closes early, and on the third day after closing it sinks beneath the water and matures seed—if so be it that it produces seed at all!

There is a great variation in the shape and size of Nymphaea flowers; some are beautifully cup-shaped, others star-shaped with long flat petals, tapering to a point, as *Nymphaea gracilis*, some species have long stiff stems, 12 to 18 inches above water, while others are flexible and the flowers float on the surface of the water. Nymphaeas have all leaves floating, but occasionally, when crowded, the leaves stand out of the water. *N. tuberosa*, one of the strongest growers, soon crowds its own foliage out of the water, and often indeed the rhizomes likewise.

The introduction of the *Victoria regia* into England gave a stimulus to aquaticulture, and many tropical Nymphaeas had reached England prior to the introduction of the Victoria, also Nelumbos; their cultivation, however, had never become general. The facts that they could not be grown out-of-doors, and that numerous tropical plants occupied the space of the greenhouse and conservatory to better advantage, were potent factors in this.

About fifty years ago the *Victoria regia* was first introduced into England, and two years later was grown in a special house erected for it by Mr. Cope, of Philadelphia; with it other tropical aquatics were introduced and this marks the commencement of the cultivation of aquatics in the United States. Little progress, however, was made; the indulgence in the new cult involved considerable labor and expense, and only the few could enjoy such a floral luxury. In 1853 Mr. John Fisk Allen, of Salem, Mass., exhibited a leaf and flower of *Victoria regia* before the Massachusetts Horticultural Society; other aquatics were also exhibited, and the cultivation of such increased somewhat, but it was not until it was found that the Egyptian Lotus, *Nelumbo nucifera,* was quite hardy that aquatic gardening commanded real attention. The introduction of that plant, as well as of several species of Nymphaea, into the public parks and gardens became general throughout the United States. At the present time [1897] exhibitions are not complete without a display of aquatic flowers, and they have ever proved to be a special feature and center of attraction wherever shown. The aquatic plants at the World's Fair [1893] in Chicago attracted considerable interest, and their cultivation has increased by rapid strides since that time.❀

From *The Water Garden* by William Tricker, 1897.

THE *VICTORIA REGIA*

The *Victoria regia* is now well known throughout the civilized world, although its introduction into England and the United States dates back to a period less than fifty years ago. It is grown most successfully in the open air, and is a very great attraction whenever seen, it is the grandest and most wonderful of all aquatic plants. It is a native of South America, where it inhabits the tranquil bays of the great streams. The earliest traveller who discovered it was Hoenke, in 1801. Dr. Lindley tells us that "Bompland subsequently met with it, but M. D'Orbigny was the first to send home specimens to Paris in 1828; they were, however, neglected or overlooked. In a work published some few years after this time, M. D'Orbigny mentions having discovered the plant in the river Parana in Guiana. It was known, he says, to the natives by the name of Irupe, in allusion to the shape of the leaves, which resemble that of the broad dishes used in the country. The Spaniards call the plant water-maize, as they collect the seeds and eat them roasted."

It was a great day, horticulturally speaking, when on the first day of January, 1837, Sir R. Schomburgk came upon this noble plant in British Guiana. A German traveller had found it in some tributaries of the Amazon in 1832, but it was when Sir R. Schomburgk, in a letter to the Royal Geographical Society of England, described the largest specimen he had met with, that public attention was drawn to this magnificent plant. Sir R. Schomburgk rightly described it as a vegetable wonder. It was while proceeding up the river Berbice that he came upon it. "It had gigantic leaves five to six feet across, with a flat broad rim, lighter green above and

Underside of leaves of Victoria amazonica (regia) shows structure that imparts buoyancy.

vivid crimson underneath, floating upon the water, and in character with such wonderful foliage I saw luxuriant flowers, each consisting of numerous petals passing in alternate tints, from pure white to rose and pink. The smooth water was covered with the blossoms, and which possess the additional charm of extensively diffusing a sweet fragrance." Its introduction to gardens is probably owing to Mr. Bridges, who, in his journey through Bolivia, found the *Victoria regia* in considerable abundance, and he brought home in 1846 seeds in wet clay, well-dried foliage, and flowers in spirits.

The first flower was produced in England in November of 1849, and was presented to Her Majesty, Queen Victoria, in whose honor the plant was named. Its gigantic leaves are five to six feet in diameter, turned up at the edges, five to seven inches additional. The upper surface is of a deep brilliant green, the under side a vivid crimson, and furnished with strong veins which are cellular, filled with air, and form a regular and elegant network. The underside of the leaf, as well as the foot stalks of the leaves and flowers, are covered with very prominent and elastic spines. The peculiar formation of the under surface of the leaf impart to it great buoyancy, rendering the mature leaf capable of bearing a considerable weight, not infrequently 150 to 200 pounds, and a plant grown at Tower Grove Park, St. Louis, in 1896, had a leaf that bore the unprecedented weight of 250 pounds. A Victoria was grown at Clifton, N.J., which had at one time twenty perfect leaves in different stages of development, and which produced a large number of its magnificent flowers from July to October. These flowers are not less marvelous than the leaves; when expanded a bloom measures from fifteen to eighteen inches in diameter, the petals are very numerous, the color, when the bud first opens, is white, passing by successive shades, the second day, into a rosy hue, a lively red to crimson. The flowers exhale a pleasant odor, not unlike that of a rich pineapple, during the first evening on opening; this is distinctly perceptible as soon as the sepals show signs of bursting, and hours before the flower is open. The bloom lasts but two days, or more correctly speaking, two nights, during the hot weather, but occasionally at the end of the season the flowers endure three days.

Photo by Elvin McDonald

Later it became a difficult matter to obtain seed of the true *V. regia*, and being desirous of securing it I determined to try a new field for supply, and during the winter, 1893-94, received from a European house some seed purporting to be of the true *Victoria regia*. Some of this was sown about the 10th of March under precisely the same conditions as other Victoria seed, and in water at a temperature of 85 degrees to 90 degrees Fahrenheit. After waiting a month and seeing no signs of germination, I gave up hopes of securing a plant for that season; but at the same time I examined another portion of the same lot of seed which had not been subjected to a higher temperature than that of the house, and was greatly surprised to find several had germinated. The seedlings were potted off singly, and treated as other young Victoria plants; subjected to a temperature of 85 degrees, and re-potted at intervals until planted in permanent quarters on May 20.

From the first these seedlings exhibited a feature which marked them as entirely distinct from the original form, the leaves being light green and mottled with reddish brown on the face, purplish below. The rapid growth and the early cupping of the leaf were also very noticeable. In its permanent quar-

Lotus

ters the growth of the plant was still more remarkable, and it was soon evident it would outrun the older plants of the other variety, which in fact it did, at a very early date. The first flower was produced about July 15, and during August the same plant produced twelve magnificent flowers; these on first opening were pure white, and on the second day of a lively rose color. At one time as many as nine flowers and buds were visible in different stages of development, while var. Randii produced but half that number, and seldom had more than five presentable leaves at one time.

The same characteristics of the plant have been manifest during the past two seasons, and it has exhibited a tendency to flower at a very early stage. Last year a few plants that were not wanted were allowed to remain in eight-inch pots, where they produced flower buds and one perfect flower, and would have continued to flower had they not been removed. Last season one plant of this variety produced some pods of seed, one of which bursted earlier than was expected, and not having been bagged the seed was scattered. So far as was possible the seeds were picked up, but a number escaped notice and sank. Early in July, 1897, a number of seedling Victoria plants made their appearance on the surface of the water (which is about two feet deep).

During the winter but little water remained in the pond, and at one time what was there must have been frozen nearly solid; in spring the water was drawn off, the bottom, consisting of pure stiff clay, was pounded firm, and a layer of sand put upon it; the young plants referred to above are firmly rooted in the clay bottom and have every appearance of being strong and vigorous.

The partiality for a comparatively low temperature is a remarkable feature of this variety (which we distinguish provisionally as "Tricker's variety"). In no case has seed germinated when subjected to a temperature of 85 degrees to 95 degrees; it enjoys a temperature similar to that which is usually afforded tender Nymphaeas, and there can be no doubt whatever but that it will become a universal favorite, as it can be grown successfully under precisely the same conditions as the tender Nymphaeas.

Another variety of *Victoria regia* is recognized in England as Dixon's and is characterized by the deep coloring of its flowers.

Thus far we have records of at least three distinct forms beyond the type, but so far their exact standing has not been determined. Provisionally classed as varieties of Schomburgh's original plant, it may be that at least one of them is worthy of specific distinction, but that can only be determined on a fuller and longer acquaintance.

Water lily

Victoria regia is of easy culture; coming from a tropical country, it requires a summer temperature all the season, to grow it successfully. In its native habitat, it is a perennial, but with us, the best method is to treat it as an annual. It forms no tuber, nor rhizome, as do Nymphaeas. It produces seed freely, and if the season be sufficiently long, or if artificial heat be supplied, the seed will ripen, but it takes from two to three months to ripen the seed. After it is ripe, it should be kept in water continuously, and in a temperature not below 60 degrees.

The seed should be sown during February and March, according to the section of the country, or facilities for growing the plants. The water temperature for starting the seed should be 85 degrees to 90 degrees; the seed sown in pots, or seed pans and placed in shallow water, will develop the seedlings in about twenty days, although occasionally, some will make an appearance in ten days. These should be potted off singly into thumb pots as soon as the second leaf appears; the water temperature for potted plants need not exceed 85 degrees; the young plants should be repotted at intervals, keeping them steadily growing until they are planted out in their summer quarters. Sufficient room must be given at all times, so that the leaves are not crowded so as to overlap each other.❀

From *The Water Garden* by William Tricker, 1897.

11

ON THE CORRECT NAME FOR THE
ROYAL WATER LILY

GHILLEAN T. PRANCE

Although we tend to think of the Royal water lily as *Victoria regia*, technically this is incorrect. In fact, since 1850, according to the rules of the "International Code of Botanical Nomenclature," it should have been called *Victoria amazonica*.

The reason for this is that the first botanist to collect and describe this plant was E.F. Poeppig, the German explorer who, in 1936, named it *Euryale amazonica*. This placed the species in a genus of water lilies, *Euryale*, known previously only in China and Southeast Asia.

At about the same time Richard Schomburgk, in his pioneering exploration of British Guiana, collected this same species. The material from the Schomburgk expedition was studied and described by British botanist John Lindley who thought it to be both a new genus and species. Thus in 1837 Lindley named this most majestic of all water lilies *Victoria regia* after Queen Victoria.

A few years later in 1850 James DeCarle Sowerby, a British botanist, realized that the names *Euryale amazonica* Poeppig and *Victoria regia* Schomburgk referred to the same species. He also thought that the two genera *Euryale* and *Victoria* were different.

Accordingly, he proposed that the genus *Euryale* be used only for the single Asiatic species and that the South American species be kept in the genus *Victoria*. However, according to the code of nomenclature the oldest specific epithet or species name must be applied to any species. Since the epithet "*amazonica*" was given to the species in 1836, just one year before the name "*regia*" was used by Lindley, Sowerby made what is called a new nomenclatural combination. He combined the genus named *Victoria* with the older specific name *amazonica*. Hence the correct name for the species is *Victoria amazonica* (Poeppig) J. DeC. Sowerby. This is not a recent nomenclatural correction since it dates back to 1850, but people in general have been reluctant to give up the elegant name *Victoria regia*. With the correct name of *V. amazonica* at least the Queen is still honored by the generic name and the species is more appropriately named for the region to which it is native.

Fortunately, there are no such nomenclatural complications for the other species of the genus *Victoria, V. cruziana*, the Santa Cruz water lily, a native of Argentina.❧

GHILLEAN T. PRANCE, *former Senior Vice President for Science and Director of the Institute of Economic Botany at The New York Botanical Garden, currently is Director of The Royal Botanic Gardens, Kew.*

Tropical water lily

Lotus blossom

TROPICAL WATER LILIES IN THE
HOME WATER GARDEN

MARILYN LEDOUX

The tropical water lily is one of the most beautiful plants that can be grown in the home water garden. It is very floriferous, blooming from early summer until frost, and it comes in a wide range of vibrant colors including red, pink, blue, purple, yellow, green, white, and autumn shades. The large and quite fragrant flowers are held 6 to 18 inches above the water and are striking both from a distance and up close. The

MARILYN LEDOUX, *Curator of Special Plant Collections, Missouri Botanical Garden, St. Louis.*

tropical water lily also has beautiful foliage which can be either lush green or mottled.

Tropical water lilies are relatively easy to grow, their main requirements being full sun, rich soil, and warm, quiet water.

Light

Full or nearly full sun is very important because the more sun the water lily receives, the more blooms it will produce. Water lilies should not be grown at all unless at least 5 to 6 hours of full sun can

13

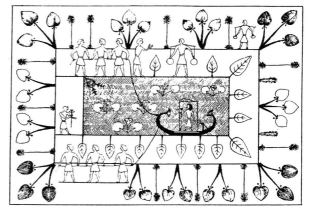

be provided each day. Sunlight is also very important for warming the water.

Soil and Containers

At least one-half bushel (16 quarts) of soil should be used for each tropical water-lily plant. Heavy garden soil is ideal. Mix three parts of soil with one part of well-rotted cow manure. Fertilizer specially blended for water lilies is also available from commercial water-lily growers. Use at recommended rate.

Planting

Once the soil has been prepared, the water lily should be planted so that its crown is just above the soil line. Then cover the soil with sand or pea gravel to crown level and slowly submerge the container into the water. The sand or gravel helps prevent the soil from clouding the water. Water lilies may also be planted in containers that are already submerged. Just press the roots into the soil until the crown is at soil level. It is important never to cover the crown with soil. Depth from water surface to crown of plant should be approximately 4 to 12 inches.

When To Plant

Tropical water lilies should be planted only when the water temperature reaches 70 degrees F or above. Planting before this time can result in dormancy and a long delay before growth resumes. In St. Louis, water temperature will usually reach 70 degrees in late May. Localities farther north of St. Louis will be correspondingly later and localities south, earlier.

Summer Care

Feeding water lilies two to three times during the summer will result in more and larger blooms. Commercial fertilizer tablets pressed into the soil around the water lily are easiest to use. Granular fertilizer such as 12-12-12 lawn food may also be used. Place a handful in a small paper bag or newspaper and press into the soil around the roots on two sides of the plant.

Optional summer care includes removing any old, yellowing leaves or spent blooms.

Pests

Tropical water lilies are relatively pest-free. Occasionally they will get aphids, caterpillars, or worms. Aphids can often be controlled by hosing them off the leaves. For more severe infestations, aphids can be controlled with any insecticide that lists controlling aphids on its label. Use care if fish are in the pool. Caterpillars and worms are best controlled with the biological insecticides Dipel or Thuricide. These are harmless to fish.

Winter Care

For most people, tropical water lilies are best treated as annuals and purchased new each year. However, the containers of water lilies can be kept in a greenhouse pool over winter. The plants will probably go dormant, because of the cooler water, but should resume growth when the water warms up again in the spring.

Varieties

There are two types of tropical water lilies—day bloomers and night bloomers. Day bloomers open in the morning and close in the late afternoon or evening. Night bloomers open in the evening and remain open until midmorning on sunny days, longer on cloudy ones. Day bloomers come in blue, purple, pink, yellow, red, green, white, and autumn shades. My favorite varieties include 'Baghdad' (blue), 'Persian Lilac' (pink), 'Evelyn Randig' (magenta-rose), 'Green Smoke' (green), and 'Albert Greenberg' (yellow-and-pink bi-color). Night bloomers are only available in red, pink, and white. My favorites are 'Red Flare' (red), 'Mrs. George C. Hitchcock' (pink), and 'Missouri' (white). ❀

Sources

Lilypons Water Gardens
Lilypons, MD 21717

or

Brookshire, TX 77423

Slocum Water Gardens
1101 Cypress Gardens Rd.
Winter Haven, FL 33880

Van Ness Water Gardens
2460 N. Euclid Avenue
Upland, CA 91786

Waterford Gardens
74 Allendale Ave.
Saddle River, NJ 07458

William Tricker, Inc.
7125 Tanglewood Dr.
P.O. Box 7843
Independence, OH 44131

Lotus (Nelumbo nucifera) in BBG's lily pools.

'Director George Moore', a tropical water lily, growing in a tub — part of a terrace garden.

A Small Garden Pool for
Hardy Water Lilies

Judith E. Hillstrom

Create a new dimension in your garden landscape with a simple tub pool and a hardy water lily. Within this Lilliputian world your imagination can come alive. Add goldfish for splashes of color, watch frogs who may come to visit, fall under the charm of a floating water-lily blossom. What a delight on a midsummer's day!

There is a magic and fascination in water gardening, and with planning and some dedicated work your fantasy can become reality. To begin, use the hardy water lilies' cultural requirements as a guide in choosing the site for a garden pool. Selecting the correct spot is the most important consideration, since proper exposure is critical. An ideal location in which to grow water lilies is one which receives sun all day. A minimum of four hours sunlight produces lush foliage but few

JUDITH E. HILLSTROM, *St. Paul, Minnesota, has been a free-lance writer and gardener for over 20 years.*

blossoms. Where shade is a problem, more bloom can be encouraged with judicious pruning of overhead foliage. Water-lily bud development will be regulated in direct proportion to the amount of sun it receives.

A Simple Tub Pool

When we think of a garden pool, pictures come to mind of those gracing the lawns of stately mansions. However, such limitations as space and modest budgets necessitate a more practical approach. A prudent alternative, in terms of cost, is the tub pool which can be placed singly or in a group. With the proper framework and attractive plantings, a common washtub can be transformed into a miniature water garden.

Galvanized washtubs were manufactured in three shapes: round, square, and oblong—measuring 23 inches in diameter, 22 inches square, and 42 inches long, respectively. The depth of all sizes is 12 inches. Although metal washtubs are not readily available in stores nowadays, they may be found in Grandmother's cellar or perhaps at a garage sale. A bit of hunting may bring success and can add to the adventure.

With tub in hand and the location selected, work can begin. Turn the tub upside-down on the site after clearing away all grass, plants, and debris. Using a pointed instrument, sketch an outline of the inverted container in the soil. Lift off the washtub and dig the hole within the outline. Make the opening slightly larger than the marking on the ground. These few inches are needed to jockey the tub into position. Permanent placing should be approximately one inch above ground level to avoid soil washing into the pool after watering and rainstorms.

Lower the tub into the open hole. Rest a board across the rim for a carpenter's level. When tub is level, put dry sand into crevices and gaps between the earth wall and side of tub. This will hold the tub in place. Sand is used, particularly in the north, as a safeguard against the heaving caused by winter thaws. Tamp the sand firmly around the tub using a broad, wedge-shaped stick. After the narrow space is filled, scoop out a small trough around the tub's rim. This small moat prevents unwanted elements from slipping into the pool.

This washtub is your future pool and when it has settled in, you may disguise the galvanized rim. Brick and mortar is formal; while at the other extreme, natural or tinted gravel might be spread as a ground cover intermingled with trailing plants. I used flat limestone. The irregular pieces of rock were chosen in sizes that could be handled easily. Stones were placed in the earth around the perimeter of the galvanized tub. Set the stones so that they extend toward the center a few inches beyond the rim edge. Patience is required to fit the stones together so the tub edge is concealed and the arrangement attractive.

A word about the life expectancy of galvanized washtubs: metal tubs withstand the rigors of natural elements quite well, but after ten years or so, check for leaks each spring prior to planting. Fill the tub with water and let stand several hours. Watch for a point where the water stops receding. Side seams may widen and begin to leak. These leaks can be plugged with caulking. When the fissure is in the tub's bottom, a coating of tar will solve the problem.

With stones in position, their tones blend into the surrounding earth. Now the washtub no longer exists. In its place there is a garden pool awaiting plants.

Hardy Water Lilies

Leaves of hardy water lilies are smooth and round, measuring four inches in diameter, in some varieties mottled with chocolate. Their flowers bloom in glistening white and in shades and hues of red, pink, and yellow.

There is a pygmy variety of hardy water lily (*Nymphaea* x *helvola*). It has two inch pads and bears blossoms a mere inch across. It is a good candidate for tub pools—two to three water lilies to a pool.

In choosing your first hardy water lily, the 'Marliac White' is the easiest to grow and longest lived; mine has survived over two decades. The red 'Gloriosa' lives not as long, yet with proper winter care its usual life span is six seasons.

Culture: Plant hardy water lilies when daytime temperatures reach 60 degrees F. Hardy types are not affected by chilly night temperatures, but guard against hard frosts as mildew will form on the crown and retard growth.

When planting water lilies, it is wisest to build a planting-box unit from old lumber, rather than to put soil and lily root directly into the bottom of the pool. When winter approaches you can lift the entire unit out and carry it to storage. A box 12 inches square by approximately seven inches deep is workable. Never use redwood as it is harmful to fish. Pygmy varieties grow well in six-inch clay pots.

Hardy water lilies are shipped bare root from mail-order nurseries specializing in water plants. Upon arrival, unwrap the rhizome; it will be black in color, elongated, and solid. At one end is the crown from which leaves and buds sprout, while fat, yellow, fleshy roots grow along each side of the tuberous rhizome. With age the rhizome enlarges, and the toughness of this hardy and succulent rhizome enables it to withstand abrupt weather changes during summers outdoors and to survive long winters.

Before planting the water-lily root, form a long mound of soil down the center of the box. This low ridge of soil will hold the rhizome with the crown in a slightly raised position. Then press the roots firmly into the planting mix. Do not cover the crown. When finished the back of the rhizome should be barely visible beneath a thin layer of soil.

After the rhizome and roots are securely anchored in the planting box, cover with a half inch of coarse brown sand or gravel to prevent muddying the water.

Use soil of heavy consistency such as fertile garden loam with clay. Do not use peat, sandy-textured material or soil from woods or swamp.

Water lilies are heavy feeders. Aquatic specialists offer a fertilizer specifically formulated for *Nymphaea* culture. Follow directions on the package of this commercial plant food—in concentrated, non-burning form it is meant to be mixed into the soil at planting time.

Pulverized, commercially bagged cow manure is used by some growers. The proportion is one part dry manure to three parts soil. Do not use fresh manure. It mucks the soil and turns water to a brown tea.

Filling the Pool

Place the planted box in the bottom of the pool. When filling the pool after the box is in place, anchor the end of the hose at pool bottom, positioned so the trickle of water is aimed toward the metal wall. Should the box shift while water is flowing, wedge a rock firmly between box and pool wall. Although you may have filled the pool brimful a few hours ago an inch or so of vacant space shows below the rim. This water was soaked up by the soil in porous planting containers. Add water as needed to compensate for evaporation. Refills are accomplished without bother at the same time you water your flower border with the garden hose. Water in the pool need not be changed unless it becomes dirty.

A small garden pool containing water lilies and gold fish.

Photo by Elvin McDonald

A water lily correctly planted in properly fertilized soil will begin to grow immediately. By midsummer, foliage will be lush. When lily pads tilt upright in the water, remove older leaves to permit sunlight to filter through the water. This will encourage greater bud production.

Winter Care

Winter storage of the hardy water lily is simple when you have a place where temperatures remain in the 40 degrees to 55 degrees F range such as a cool basement corner or root cellar. In autumn, prior to a hard freeze, lift the planting box from the pool and allow to drain for a few hours. Do not cut off leaves. Pack moist compost over the damp soil to keep it from drying out through winter months.

The following spring carry the lily box from its storage place out into the garden. Invert the box, shake and pry away last year's soil from the rhizome. After the rhizome is carefully cleaned, examine it for suckers. Suckers are tiny, yellowish leaves sprouting near the crown or in the tangle of roots along the side. If these are not removed the water lily will not bloom. Use a small sharp knife to cut out the sprouts.

Occasionally a sucker develops into an immature plant. Free from the parent by cutting out a half-inch wedge of rhizome with a few roots attached. Plant one to a six-inch clay pot, and plantlets will grow quickly to blooming-size. Replant the large rhizome in the planting box unit with fresh soil and fertilizer.

Goldfish and water lilies make a pleasant combination and provide a fine balance of nature. Plants release oxygen and absorb carbon dioxide, while fish work in the reverse. Each assists the other in keeping the water clean. Fish eat their fill by nibbling algae off pool walls and also consume insect larvae.

When envisioning blossoms of the water lily none wrote more eloquently than Mrs. N.E. Lovejoy in the *Journal of the Columbus Horticultural Society* of 1887: "You may look upon a mountain and wish it were loftier or more precipitous; upon a river and wish it were clearer; upon a tree and desire for it some greater spread of its boughs, some richer shadings of its foliage. But you cannot look upon a water lily and wish it to be other than it is."❀

A day-blooming water lily in BBG's lily pools.

HOW TO PLANT YOUR LILY POOL

COURTESY OF WILLIAM TRICKER INC.

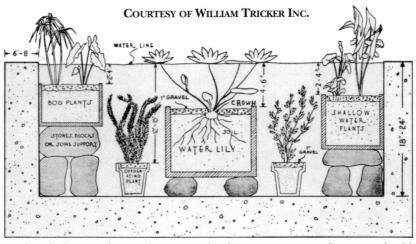

Pools with sloping sides may be arranged in this same manner. All supports should be solid and secure to avoid tipping over.

How To Plant

Water lilies are very easy to grow. Under natural conditions the roots are in rich soil in the shallow water of a marsh or pond exposed to full sunshine. These conditions are easily reproduced in the garden. In natural ponds, hardy water lilies may be planted in water from 6 to 18 inches deep and are planted simply by pressing the root into the good soil at the bottom. Small artificial pools should be at least one foot deep, allowing for six inches of water over 6 inches of soil. In larger pools use containers, either tubs or boxes, holding at least one bushel of soil. The depth of the water may be from 6 to 12 inches over the tub or container. Artificial pools need not be more than 24 inches deep. Twenty inches makes a satisfactory depth. It is best to provide a separate container for each water lily or lotus.

Do Not Drain Pool Before Planting

Prepare all the necessary containers, place them at the proper levels (see diagram) and fill the pool with water. It is preferable to plant your lilies and other aquatic plants in their containers before immersing in pool. It is important, however, that the crown on the water lily (the growing end) should not be below the surface of the gravel.

Soil

The best soil for water lilies and aquatic plants is a mixture of three parts of good top soil and one part of thoroughly rotted cow manure—a heavy clay soil is very satisfactory. Muck from swamps, soil from woods, peat moss and sand should not be used in the soil. All soil in pools should be covered with approximately one inch of clean gravel which prevents any particles from the soil floating into the water and discoloring it.

Planting

Hardy water lilies may be planted quite early in the spring but not until the water has warmed up so they will start immediately into new growth. In the latitude of Chicago, Cleveland, and New York, this date is usually toward the latter part of April. For tropical water lilies the first week in June, if weather permits, is usually the proper time in the same localities mentioned above. For points south of this line the date is, of course, earlier. Tropical water lilies especially should be planted in full sunshine and in a depth of water from 6 to 18 inches. Hardy water lilies do best in a depth of water from four to six inches and lotus in the same depth as the tropical lilies.

Lotus

Lotus rhizomes need rich soil and plenty of room. Place the rhizome in a horizontal position two inches below the surface of the soil and provide a depth of water four to six inches when first planted. After becoming well established the depth of water can be increased to a maximum of 12 inches, but an average depth of eight inches of water is ideal. Handle rhizomes carefully during unpacking and planting so that the growing end is not broken. Potted plants are usually obtainable late in the season and are simply rhizomes started into growth in pots in tanks in greenhouses and when received are planted exactly the same as tropical lilies by pressing the ball of earth into the soft mud to a position just below the surface of the gravel. ❀

HOW TO MAKE A TUB GARDEN

COURTESY OF SLOCUM WATER GARDENS

1. Choose a sunny location.

2. Sink the tub at least half-way into the soil.

3. Place four inches of good garden soil in the bottom.

4. Plant hardy water lilies horizontally.

5. Plant tropical water lilies upright.

6. Plant bog plants upright.

7. Add a half-inch of sand.

8. Spread burlap bag on top of sand. (This prevents the soil being stirred up when water is added.)

9. Fill tub with water and remove burlap.

GARDEN POOLS

Edmond O. Moulin

If a water feature is in your garden plan, begin by surveying your property. Ask yourself the following questions:

1) Where does your family relax?

2) Is this area in view from inside the house?

3) Is it protected from the street and neighbors—in other words, private?

4) How is the drainage?

When these questions have been answered and you have a general idea of where you want to locate your water feature, consider also that flowering aquatic plants perform best in full sun, so the pool should be located away from large trees. This will also lighten clean-up chores because fallen leaves can clog drains and be unsightly. It is also advantageous to follow the natural contour lines of your property and to locate the pool in the lowest area if that location meets the above criteria.

The size, shape, and location of a pool or smaller water feature is a personal matter. It can be as small as a birdbath, with a simple fountain falling into a basin with the water circulated by a small pump. Wall fountains take up even less space and still provide the sight and sound of water.

EDMOND O. MOULIN, *Brooklyn, New York. Director of Horticulture at Brooklyn Botanic Garden since coming here in 1968 from the academic world; he was weaned on practical horticulture in his father's arborist and landscape business.*

English ivy planted and trained to grow on the wall around the fountain provides contrast and adds textural interest. (The wall-mounted fountain is attached to a hidden pump and reservoir by tubing. The water is then recirculated.)

With such a small water feature there is the added dividend of winter use. As long as the water is moving the pump can be kept operating in freezing weather. Ice will create new sculptural effects. Antifreeze can be added if there is no danger to surrounding plants or fish or household pets. If the water

A naturalistic garden pool.

isn't moving, pull the plug on the pump.

Larger pools can be constructed in any size and shape. There are prefabricated pools or pools can be created from a hole covered with heavy black plastic (see p. 24) or with poured concrete. The last requires the most time, effort, and money, but is also the most long lasting. It should be kept in mind that there is maintenance involved *after* a pool of any sort is constructed, so don't be overly ambitious at the outset.

Keep in mind also that a pool is a responsibility. If there are small children in the family or the neighborhood, the pool must be fenced with a secure gate at the entrance. Many communities have ordinances regarding the height and type of fence so that it would be prudent to check before starting to build your pool.

Water features can be even more complex and ambitious. A pool fed by a stream can add interest and lend itself to bridges and waterfalls. Rocks set in concrete along the edges of larger water features provide the opportunity for interesting plantings. An assortment of groundcovers such as rockspray cotoneaster (*C. horizontalis*), pumilio mugo pine (*Pinus mugo* var. 'Pumilio'), and lily-turf (*Liriope* spp.) can be used. Creeping sedums, creeping baby's breath (*Gypsophila repens*), and annually planted alyssum (*Lobularia maritima*) also work well and provide contrasts in foliage, textures, and colors.

The addition of any water feature is a matter of personal choice. It can be large or just a small tub sunk into the ground planted with a small water lily (see p. 19). Whatever the size, the presence of water will add interest, variety and a soothing quality to your landscape.❧

DESIGN AND PREPARATION

1. Draw garden to scale on paper (an overlay will allow experimentation without destroying the plan)
2. Select sunny spot for pool away from trees that might eventually shade it
3. With plan complete outline pool on site by:
   a. using a hose to outline free-form designs
   b. 2" x 4" lumber to outline geometric forms
   c. a string line from a center point to outline circular forms
4. Check grade of site with a level
5. Clear away vegetation
6. Dig hole within outline to proper depth
7. Be certain that pool edge is at least one inch above ground level
8. Install edging: stones, gravel, and/or plantings
9. Plant pool
10. Add finish if desired

HOW TO BUILD A LILY POOL

SIMPLE POOL CONSTRUCTION—CROSS-SECTION OF CONCRETE POOL

1 Choose sunny location.
2 Dig hole with sloping sides.
3 Put pipes in place.
4. Spread 3" outer layer concrete.
5. Lay down wire.

6. Spread 3" inner layer concrete.
7. With broom, brush wet mixture of sand and cement over pool to fill crevices. (Use 2 parts sand to 1 cement.)

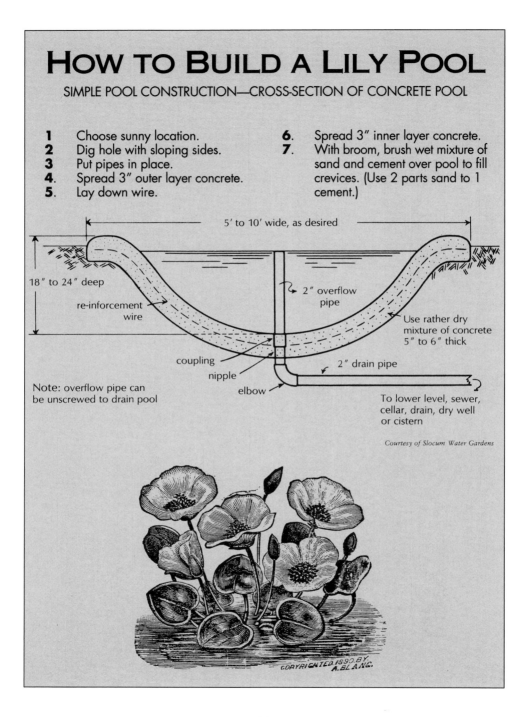

5' to 10' wide, as desired

18" to 24" deep

re-inforcement wire

2" overflow pipe

Use rather dry mixture of concrete 5" to 6" thick

coupling
nipple
elbow

2" drain pipe

Note: overflow pipe can be unscrewed to drain pool

To lower level, sewer, cellar, drain, dry well or cistern

Courtesy of Slocum Water Gardens

COPYRIGHTED 1890 BY A. BLANC.

PROPAGATING WATER LILIES AND AQUATICS

Peter D. Slocum

Aquatic plants reproduce themselves rapidly and prolifically. This is often true in locations where we may not want such abundance—for example, the infamous water hyacinth (*Eichhornia crassipes*) and hydrilla (*Hydrilla verticillata*), which are scourges of public waterways in the southern states. The opposite can seem to be true in regard to the lovely varieties that we enjoy in our garden pools, but propagation of aquatic plants is not a difficult task limited to commercial growers.

Water lilies (*Nymphaea* spp.) are divided into two major types, tropical and hardy, treated here as separate subjects because their physical characteristics are different.

Tropical Water Lilies

Tropical water lilies are the largest, showiest plants for the garden pool with flowers colors ranging through the spectrum. In the Deep South in protected locations many varieties continue to grow and bloom all year. Elsewhere they can be planted when water temperatures reach 70

PETER D. SLOCUM, *owner of Slocum Water Gardens, Winter Haven, Florida, is a writer and lecturer on all phases of water gardening.*

Aquatic animals and marsh plants, 1558.

degrees F and above. For most of the country this is generally sometime between the middle of May and the middle of June. Once established, they continue to grow in size and to flower until water temperatures fall below 60 degrees in the autumn when the decline in temperature induces dormancy.

Dormancy is triggered by the cooling down of the water. Instead of the water lily utilizing its strength to produce new leaves and flowers, all energies are diverted toward the formation of a tuber to store starches and carbohydrates. As the process advances all apparent evidence of life subsides. Blooming stops and leaf size diminishes. When the cycle is complete, the plant will appear to have died.

Dig carefully into the soil at the center of the container for the tuber. This tuber serves as a storage capsule for wintering the resting plant. As long as it remains safely submerged and not frozen, the plant will remain viable. Tubers can be stored indoors in the more extreme climates. Cover the tuber with damp sand, sawdust, or vermiculite. Moisten the material and store in a cool place. Whether left in the planting container or removed, the resting plant will not require light. Use tubers the size of English walnuts for propagating in the spring.

When water temperatures rise in the spring, remove the tubers from storage and pot them in good topsoil (no fertilizer at this time) in shallow water. New leaf growth will soon appear. When surface leaves are two to three inches across, you should be able to remove the new plantlet from the tuber. Leave the tuber in place in the soil. Do not force the removal of the plantlets; wait a few more days, until separation can be easily made. More than one plantlet may be produced. Pot each individually in small pots (four to six inches) using topsoil enriched with a well-balanced (10-10-10) fertilizer (one teaspoon mixed in the bottom half of the pot). In a few weeks the young plants will be ready to transplant to a bushel-size box or tub (32 qts.) or directly planted into earth-bottom ponds for the season.

Some excellent varieties which easily propagate from tubers are:

'Albert Greenberg'. Orange flowers with heavily mottled leaf patterns; blooms prolifically. One of the best.

'Director George T. Moore'. This one is a vigorous grower with darker blue flowers; it generally winters well and produces several blooms at a time.

'Enchantment'. Best of the large pink flowered lilies. Opens earlier in the day than most other day-blooming tropicals.

'Evelyn Randig'. Flower color close to 'Red Beauty' with beautiful leaves.

'King of Blues'. Large flowers of dark blue. Easy to grow.

'Mrs. George C. Hitchcock'. Largest of the night-bloomers with huge pink blossoms and tough, somewhat bronzed, leaves.

'Pamela'. Full-size lily with flowers of light blue and mottled leaves.

'Red Beauty'. Closest shade we have to a red in day-blooming tropical water lilies. Propagates easily.

'Red Flare'. Most popular red night-blooming lily. Flowers and leaves are deep wine red. Most compact grower of the night-blooming water lilies.

'St. Louis'. All of the good features of 'Yellow Dazzler' with pastel yellow flowers.

'Ted Uber'. Beautiful white flowers; tough plant. Definitely the best day-blooming white.

'Trudy Slocum'. Best of the white night-bloomers. Excellent in every way with large pure white flowers.

'Yellow Dazzler'. Deepest yellow flower, a strong growing plant. Best of the deep yellows with all of the good points we look for in choosing a water lily.

The last two lilies on this list are night-blooming, which means that they begin

Eichhornia crassipes

blooming at dusk, continue through the night and do not stop at dawn. The blossoms last until late in the morning. It is not unusual for them to continue until nearly noon each day. Night-bloomers can be propagated from tubers. Night-bloomers also reproduce during the season by vegetative means. Young plants are formed around the base of the parent plant, giving the impression of a mass of small leaves. These plantlets can be transplanted as desired without waiting for dormancy.

Some special water lilies, all day-blooming tropicals, can be propagated through the formation of perfect miniatures of the parent plant at the leaf petiole. These are known as viviparous species. They are among the most interesting to propagate. This phenomenon occurs in fairly small varieties of blue and purple hues. 'Dauben', 'Panama Pacific', 'August Koch', and 'Mrs. Martin E. Randig' are the choices most commonly available. All are good. As the young plant begins to form you should notice a furry-appearing protrusion swelling at the point where the leaf is attached to the stem. This will enlarge into a small leaf formation as the parent plant leaf begins the process of decomposition. In ideal conditions the baby plant may

form and bloom while still attached to the parent leaf. In ponds with soil bottoms, the plantlets will settle to the bottom and root. Or the leaves may be placed on soil-filled pots just under the water surface so that the roots may enter the soil as growth progresses. The plant may be transplanted after a few weeks. Leaves may also be removed from parent stock before the plantlets are fully formed and floated in water where they will continue to develop before planting.

Tropicals from Seed

Some water-lily varieties will form seed pods. The base of the flower will enlarge following the completion of bloom, if seed is set. Collect seedpods and allow them to ripen in a jar or pail of water until the pod breaks. After breaking, the fleshy parts of the seedpod will rapidly decompose and in a few days the seeds can be cleaned and dried. Pour the contents of the container through a fine mesh screen. (Water-lily seeds are very tiny so the gauge of the screen must be fine enough to prevent the seed from passing through. Fine window screen can be used.) Sow seeds in soil and place in shallow water. The tender seedlings will appear soon after sowing and then can be transplanted. Seed can be sown directly into soil-bottom ponds or the seedpods may be left on the plants and allowed to self-sow. Stored dried seed will remain viable for a couple of seasons.

Victoria amazonica, the giant water lily of the Amazon River, is an example of a water lily that reproduces solely by seed. An annual that does not form tubers or produce any vegetative plantlets, its leaves are over six feet across. It blooms at night with flowers of 12 to 15 inches or more and covers surfaces exceeding 30 feet. The seeds are hard-shelled orbs about the size of the common garden pea and generally take two years to sprout. Collect the seeds in the same manner previously described, except store them in water. Second-year seed should be sown in large containers of soil or, preferably, directly into the water of the pond where they will germinate and grow to a transplanting size. Victorias are among the most tropical of water lilies and require temperatures above 70 degrees F to germinate and sustain growth. They are most impressive from late summer through the autumn when seeds are formed. Treat them as annuals.

Hardy Water Lilies

These differ from tropicals in that the tuber structure is a permanent part of the root system. In hardy varieties this tuberous structure is a rhizome, a thick fleshy root storage system that stores food for dormancy. The plant forms a clump which can be lifted and divided into several plants and should be divided every two or three years.

Hardy water lilies are frequently chosen for their strong colors. Some of the best varieties over the years have been:

'Attraction'. Large, red-flowered; easily grown throughout the country. Forms clumps in ponds and in large containers in pools.

'Comanche'. The larger version of the orange hardy lilies. An old favorite.

'Fabiola'. An excellent pink flower. It will remain small for tub garden use or grow to full size in larger spaces.

'Queen of Whites'. An improved pure white for use in pools of all sizes.

'Sioux'. A changeable orange flower of fairly small size. Opens yellow and grows darker with the passage of the days.

'Sunrise'. The largest-flowering yellow hardy lily. Starts early in the spring with numerous blooms most of the summer.

'Yellow Pygmy' (*Nymphaea* x *helvola*). A true dwarf variety. Excellent for limited spaces such as tub gardens.

Lotus

The next major group of aquatics that can be easily propagated is the lotus (*Nelumbo* spp.). Lotus are cold-hardy plants that grow and winter well throughout the country if their rootstocks do not freeze. These plants grow above the water's surface to four to five feet. This species is a vigorous grower that should not be planted in a pond or lake bottom where it will take over. They are best planted in large containers in pools or ponds. Rhizomes resemble a large banana and are formed in the soil in abundance as dormancy approaches. New plants can be started from rhizomes or seed. The seeds are very hardcoated and must be scarified (abraded) to germinate. In nature, lotus seeds remain viable but unsprouted for many years until chemical or bacterial action softens them. Scarification cuts the time to a few days. To scarify the seeds file the outer seed coat enough to weaken it so that water may enter. Use care not to file too deeply. Stop filing at the very first indication of the white inside. Sow the prepared seed in containers of soil. They will plant themselves as they sprout.

Other Aquatics

Shallow-water plants and bog plants can also be propagated in the home garden pool. Water iris, pickerel weed, giant papyrus, and other aquatics can be propagated by division. The umbrella palm and dwarf papyrus can be reproduced by dividing the roots of established clumps. Several of the shallow-water and bog aquatics multiply by runners spreading under the soil. Cattail, taro, and arrowhead are examples of this type. Most will also form

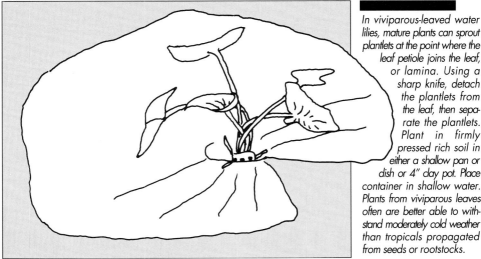

In viviparous-leaved water lilies, mature plants can sprout plantlets at the point where the leaf petiole joins the leaf, or lamina. Using a sharp knife, detach the plantlets from the leaf, then separate the plantlets. Plant in firmly pressed rich soil in either a shallow pan or dish or 4" clay pot. Place container in shallow water. Plants from viviparous leaves often are better able to withstand moderately cold weather than tropicals propagated from seeds or rootstocks.

viable seed that can be collected for later planting or left to seed themselves.

Floating and oxygenating plants are the remaining plants that complete the garden pool. They are among the most important in the overall scheme of things in the great benefits they provide their aquatic environment. The floating plants such as water lettuce (*Pistia stratiotes*) and duckweed (*Lemna*) provide surface shading which helps reduce algae problems by blocking sunlight at the water's surface. Algae grow in sunlight and use the available nutrients for survival. Therefore keeping down algae is important in helping further pool balance.

Even more important than floating plants are the oxygenating plants which grow under the surface of the water. Plants such as *Anacharis, Cabomba*, marestail, *Vallisneria*, and several of the submerged sagittarias are beneficial. They are effective in controlling the quality of the water by absorbing nutrients and carbon dioxide and releasing oxygen into the water as a by-product of photosynthesis (the sunlight-function-to-food of

plant leaves). Murky waters clear in a surprisingly short time when oxygenating plants are at work. *Anacharis* and *Cabomba* can be propagated by cuttings of the growing tips. They are soft plants that root in a few days when potted in containers of soil in the bottom of the pool. They will also do well if simply weighted down to hold them in place. The marestail (*Ceratophyllum demersum*) can be dropped into the pool and remains neither planted nor floating but rather suspended in the pool depths. Its multibranched structure continues to grow and may be broken into new plants. The vallisnerias and sagittarias require planting in soil either in containers or directly in the bottom of soil-bottom pools and ponds. They multiply by soil-bound runners and fill in spaces between them much like the grasses in a lawn. The rapid growth of these plants accounts for their success in ridding the water of much of the problem algae, as well as being attractive. The oxygenating plants and the water lilies and floating plants are all important in balancing the conditions of the pool.❀

INSTALLATION OF A POOL LINER

1. Lay a hose or rope to the required shape and size of the pool. Commence digging, but always cut inside the finished outline to allow for final trimming and shaping.

2. The excavation is started leaving marginal shelves 9" below water level and 9-12" wide (or wider) where required for shallow water plants. In addition, the pool edge should be cut back sufficiently to accommodate the edging.

3. Short wooden pegs are inserted 3-4' apart around the pool and tops of the pegs leveled

using a spirit level. The top edge of the pool must be level because the water will show immediately any faults.

After final trimming and shaping has been completed, the depth and width of marginal shelves should be checked. The sides and base of the excavation must be closely inspected for any sharp stones or roots.

4. A cushion of sand 1/2" deep should be placed on the bottom of the excavation. Sand should then be worked into the sides of the

excavation to fill any holes and crevices which may have been made digging out stones.

The finished excavation should be neat and trim because any irregularities will show after the liner is fitted. On particularly stony ground, building grade polyethylene should be underlaid as an added precaution.

Note in the photo the lighter color of the sand.

5. The pool liner should be draped loosely into the excavation with an even overlap all around. Stones or blocks should be placed on the corners and along the sides.

6. Begin filling with water. As the pool fills, the stones should be eased off at intervals to allow the liner to fit snugly into the excavation. Some creasing is inevitable, but some of the creases can be removed by stretching and fitting as the pool fills. When full, the surplus lining can be cut off leaving a 4-5" flap. This flap can be temporarily secured by pushing 4" nails through the lining and into the ground.

7. Rectangular pools can be edged with pre-cast paving. Informal pools can be edged with broken slabs or natural stone paving. Edging should be laid on a bed of mortar mixed three parts sand to one part cement.

8. Ideally pools should be emptied before planting and stocking with fish, and this is imperative if concrete has been dropped into the water during the construction work.
Fountains, lighting and other adornments can be added during or after construction.❧

Courtesy of Stapeley Water Gardens, Stapeley, England, and Lilypons Water Gardens, Lilypons, MD.

A Portfolio of

Water and

Waterside

Plants & Gardens

Photo by Bob Scherer

This fountain is a sculpture that creates patterns of water as it rises and falls upon the pool surface.

Photo by Elvin McDonald

The centerpiece of this garden at Butchart Gardens in Victoria, B.C., is a fountain in a pool with aquatic plants. Far right: Hibiscus palustris.

Photo by Peter K. Nelson

37

Photo by Bob Scherer

38

Iris pseuda-
corus *and*
Myosotis *grow-
ing in a moist
area at Old
Westbury
Gardens. Far
left: Asiatic
Lotus.*

A pool with a naturalistic waterfall contains water hyacinth and water lilies. Far Right: 'Momo Botan' lotus.

Photo by Bob Scherer

41

to keep the ponds at the right clearness. If left to themselves, the ponds simply become so cloudy that the fish cannot be seen. This has to be closely monitored as too much chlorine could have an adverse effect on the fish.

Types of Water Plants

A number of different water plants may be found in the garden, including *Nymphaea* spp., *Nelumbo* spp., and an assortment of shallow water plants (see accompanying chart). The nymphaeas are tropical water lilies grown for their beautiful flowers and speckled leaves. These tropicals flower as long as the water temperature stays above 70 degrees F and hold their leaves in the winter if the water temperature stays above 60 degrees. The ponds generally look weak in the winter (January through March)

44

Water Gardening at Walt Disney World

Thomas W. Underwood

Water gardens complement many of our unique landscapes at the Walt Disney World Resort. Various water plants may be found in natural and cultivated settings across the property, but our foremost display is at the China Pavilion in Epcot Center. In this garden, water plants and fish thrive in two large ponds capture the peace and beauty of a Chinese garden.

Pond Construction and Design

The two ponds are made of poured concrete four inches thick. Each one is forty-five feet wide and sixty feet long. They are separated by a twenty foot concrete walkway with three PVC pipes (six inch diameter) connecting the two below water level. The height of the sides varies from two to three feet, maintaining a water level of eighteen inches. Limestone rocks two to six feet in diameter were used along the edges and in the center of the ponds to help soften the

Thomas W. Underwood *is Manager of Parks Horticulture Services at the Walt Disney World Resort. Dee Ganna, Landscape Supervisor for the China Pavilion at EPCOT Center, helped compile the information for the article.*

concrete edges and provide interest. This jagged edge with its many nooks and crannies makes the pond seem larger. Making the small seem large is one of the principles of Chinese design.

Another principle of Chinese design is the use of sound. The garden is a reflective place with its stillness interrupted only by subtle natural sounds, such as rustling leaves or trickling water. This effect is achieved by a small waterfall located at the end of the south pond. A mound of rocks three to four feet above pond elevation forms a pool. This simulated spring flows down a series of embankments for twenty feet until it spills into the pond. This scene is observed from a three-foot-wide arched walkway that crosses the stream. Both ponds are surrounded by this walkway, which allows the observer an assortment of views and moods.

Water Management

Since the two ponds are connected by PVC pipe, they are treated as one in maintaining water quality and quantity. Water is added at the waterfall and recirculated through a series of filters and skimmers and pumped back to the top of the falls. One twelve-inch skimmer is located in each pond and cleaned daily of debris. In the bottom of each pond is a two-foot metal grate drain with a wire screen to help catch leaves and twigs.

To offset evaporation and leakage, make-up water is added at the pump. This valve is always left slightly open. If too much water is ever added, whether by this valve or rain, it is discharged through two overflow pipes that stand eighteen inches from the pond's bottom. Another benefit of this continual renewal of water is

WATER PLANTS AT THE CHINA PAVILION

Name	Flower	Time of Flowering	Distinguishing Characteristics
Cyperus alternifolius	(insignificant)		Upright stems to 4 feet tall topped by umbrella-like leaves
Eleocharis dulcis	(insignificant)		Upright cylindrical foliage to 2 feet
Nelumbo nucifera 'Alba Grandiflora'	White	Day	Deep green leaves on tall stalks look like inverted umbrellas; large single flowers
Nelumbo 'Speciosum'	Pink	Day	Concave leaves on tall stalks; large pink flowers; very fragrant
Nymphaea 'August Koch'	Blue	Day	Viviparous (plantlets produced from mature leaves); huge green leaves; blue flowers with yellow centers
Nymphaea 'Director George T. Moore'	Purple-blue	Day	Leaves flecked with purple; deep violet flowers with gold centers
Nymphaea 'Mrs. George H. Pring'	Creamy white	Day	12 inch star-shaped flowers; large faintly mottled leaves; large growth habit
Nymphaea 'Pamela'	Blue	Day	Large sky blue flowers 10-12" in diameter; Leaves marbled with chestnut brown; flowers are held high above leaves
Nymphaea 'Trudy Slocum'	White	Night	Large flowers held above leaves
Pontederia cordata	Blue		Spreading; glossy olive-green heart-shaped leaves on 2-foot stems; flowers borne on spikes
Sagittaria montevidensis	White		Huge arrowhead-shaped leaves on tall stalks to 4 feet tall; flowers borne on spikes

to keep the ponds at the right clearness. If left to themselves, the ponds simply become so cloudy that the fish cannot be seen. This has to be closely monitored as too much chlorine could have an adverse effect on the fish.

Types of Water Plants

A number of different water plants may be found in the garden, including *Nymphaea* spp., *Nelumbo* spp., and an assortment of shallow water plants (see accompanying chart). The nymphaeas are tropical water lilies grown for their beautiful flowers and speckled leaves. These tropicals flower as long as the water temperature stays above 70 degrees F and hold their leaves in the winter if the water temperature stays above 60 degrees. The ponds generally look weak in the winter (January through March)

44

but make a rapid comeback in spring with the addition of a slow-release fertilizer. Loss of water plants due to cold weather has varied from no loss up to 30-40 percent. New tubers are added as needed in the spring with no real loss to the garden.

The nelumbos, or water lotus, have long-petioled leaves that are held upright out of the water. This helps add a vertical element to the pond, as the nymphaea pads lie flat on the water surface. Also, the nelumbos are not only attractive during flowering but produce an ornate seedpod afterwards. These have proven to be valuable in dried flower arrangements. The nelumbo tuber is completely hardy and comes back every spring.

Goldfish

The cultivation of fish in the ponds plays an integral part in the overall character of the garden. Their subtle movements are intriguing and enjoyable to all. Two types of goldfish, Fantail and Comet, were added to the ponds initially. Our present population is now at about three hundred.

Plant Maintenance

Each planting tub measures 24 inches wide by 10-1/2 inches deep and contains one or two water lilies. They are planted in an organic soil with a two-inch layer of white sand on top. Generally we anticipate that the lilies will need to be repotted every two to three years.

Weekly, fishing waders are donned to remove dead leaves and spent blossoms. These are cut rather than pulled so as not to injure the main plant. Most of the flowers last four to five days.

Above: Water lilies are planted in tubs and placed in the pool.
Opposite page, top: The pool at the China Pavilion, Epcot Center.
Opposite page, bottom: Another view of the China Pavilion.

All of the plants in the garden are fertilized during the spring as the weather turns warm and growth resumes. Slow-release fertilizer tablets are used. Each tub is given three to five tablets depending on the size of the plant. In July and August, during the heat of summer, growth is rapid. As water lilies readily show nutritional deficiencies, regular fertilization is important. Keeping the plants in active growth encourages flowering and insures that we will have the best possible show for our guests. ❀

PERENNIALS FOR WET PLACES

PAMELA J. HARPER

Quite a few perennials are adapted to marshy ground, and some can be grown in shallow water. A low-lying part of the garden that remains swampy could be turned to good account by growing those perennials that, in the wild, grow along the banks of streams, the margins of ponds, or in low-lying boggy places. Most of them can also be grown in ordinary soil that does not dry out, but they are at their most luxuriant where moisture is abundantly and constantly available.

If such an area does not exist, it can be created by digging out soil to a two-foot depth, lining the hole with heavy plastic, pricking this with a garden fork so that excess water can slowly escape (it is a bog you are making, not a pond), and replacing the soil mixed half-and-half with peat moss or leafmold. If the soil is poor, add some well-rotted cow manure. Most bog plants prefer acid soil, so don't add lime. Such a plastic-lined hole can quickly be remoistened when necessary with the garden hose. On a smaller scale, you can use a sunken plastic laundry tub a foot or more deep.

If a stream runs through your garden, the moist banks provide an ideal site for

PAMELA J. HARPER, *Seaford, Virginia, is a prolific writer, lecturer, and photographer (Harper Horticultural Slide Library). Co-author with Frederick McGourty of a new book,* Perennials, *published by HP Books.*

such plants if the water level remains fairly constant, but if it alternates between stream, dry ditch, and raging torrent, it is not a suitable place for plants unless a means can be found to control the flow of water.

If a pool is to be constructed, the deep central part can be surrounded by a shallower trough with its inner edge lower than the outer one, this trough being filled with soil in which to grow bog-type plants. Plastic sheeting has made the construction of this kind of pond comparatively simple: there are excellent photographs and instructions showing how to do it in the catalogs of Lilypons Water Gardens and William Tricker, Inc. (see p. 64). Preformed pools, formal or free form, can also be bought.

Smaller Perennials

Obviously the plants chosen should be of a size in proportion with their surroundings. For the smallest pools the marsh marigold or kingcup, *Caltha palustris*, heads my list. It makes substantial but compact clumps of dark green, glossy round leaves, and in spring the bright yellow waxy flowers turn it to a golden mound. *C.p.* 'Flore Pleno' is the showiest, the yellow pompoms touched with green in the middle. There is also a white form, 'Alba'.

For contrast in form try *Acorus gramineus* 'Variegatus', a Japanese sweet flag with slender, white-striped irislike leaves twelve to eighteen inches long, evergreen in the milder regions. If you like the quaint and curious, then add *Juncus effusus* 'Spiralis', an eighteen-inch rush with dark green cylindrical leaves corkscrewed as if they'd been given a permanent wave.

Irises

When we come to perennials of larger proportions, many gardeners will think first of Japanese irises (*Iris ensata*, formerly called *I. kaempferi*), so often seen displayed in shallow water in public gardens. Look closer and you'll probably find that they are being grown in pots, to facilitate removal when they go dormant and need well-drained soil. The best place for Japanese irises is a humus-rich, moist but well-drained bed or border. If you see what you think is a Japanese iris growing in water the year around, it is probably the similar two-foot *I. laevigata*, with flowers of blue, white, rose, or violet. This needs constant moisture and is at its best in a bog, or with roots under water at the pond margin. The lavender-blue flowers of *I. laevigata* 'Variegata' last no longer that any other iris—just a week or two—but the creamy-striped leaves make this one of the most lastingly decorative plants for the pondside.

The easiest of all irises to grow in boggy

soil or shallow water is the yellow flag, *I. pseudacorus*. This is not a native plant, but it has naturalized in may parts of North America and may do the same in your garden if you let seedpods form. It varies in height from two to seven feet, with single or double flowers of bright yellow, lemon, or ivory. The leaves of *I.p.* 'Variegata' are showily striped yellow in spring but turn green by midsummer. Other irises adapted to marshy ground and shallow water are *I. prismatica*, *I. versicolor*, *I. virginica*, and the species and hybrids known as Louisiana irises.

Primroses and Ligularias

Primroses are among the prettiest perenni-

47

als for boggy soil. These are not the woodland kinds, nor the ones called polyanthus, but those usually called Japanese primroses, with whorls of flowers spaced along stems from one to four feet high. Species include *Primula beesiana, P. bulleyana, P. florindae, P. helodoxa, P. japonica,* and *P. pulverulenta.* Colors include rosy pinks, crimson, yellow, orange, and purple. All flower in late spring or early summer. *P. japonica* is best known, to two feet, with flowers of white, rose, crimson, or purple. 'Miller's Crimson' and 'Postford White' are excellent selected forms. These bog-type primroses appreciate light shade, and this is essential in the hottest parts of the U.S. A lovely companion for them is the Ostrich fern, *Matteuccia struthiopteris,* a three-to-five-foot shuttlecock of ostrich-plume leaves.

All the ligularias need moist or boggy soil, otherwise the leaves wilt miserably on sunny afternoons. *L. dentata* 'Othello' and *L.d.* 'Desdemona' are similar plants, grown mainly for their hefty three- to four-foot clumps of large, heart-shaped dark green leaves with mahogany undersides. Bright orange ragged daisies open late in the season on stout branched stems. If you are of the many who don't like orange with maroon, you may prefer to remove the flowers, or grow instead *L. przewalskii, L. stenocephala,* or *L.* 'The Rocket'. These are similar and confused. They bear tall spires of yellow flowers on purple or nearly black stems over substantial clumps of jagged or deeply incised leaves.

Below: Caltha palustris, swamp marigold.
Opposite page:
Calopogon tuberosus, swamp pink.

49

AND OTHERS

The following perennials all do well in moist to wet soils:

- *Arisaema triphyllum* (Jack-in-the Pulpit) (needs shade)
- *Astilbe*
- *Chelone glabra* (Turtlehead)
- *Eupatorium fistulosum* (Goat's beard)
- *Eupatorium purpureum* (Joe-Pye weed)
- *Filipendula palmata* (Meadowsweet)
- *F. ulmaria* (Queen-of-the-Meadow)
- *Helenium autumnale* (Sneezeweed)
- *Lobelia cardinalis* (Cardinal flower)
- *Lysichiton* (Skunk cabbage) (needs light shade)
- *Lysimachia punctata* (Loosestrife)
- *Orontium aquaticum* (Golden-club)
- *Peltiphyllum peltatum* (Umbrella plant)
- *Ranunculus repens* ('Flore Pleno', double, is the most ornamental) (Butter daisy)
- *Rodgersia*
- *Sanguisorba canadensis* (Canadian burnet)
- *Trollius* (Globeflower)
- *Veratrum* (False hellebore) (light shade)
- *Vernonia* (Ironweed)
- *Zantedeschia aethiopica* (Calla lily)

All these are available either from nurseries selling perennials or from wild-flowers nurseries.

If you have a large area of untamed boggy ground, look through wildflower books for your region to find flowers you like that are sufficiently robust to compete with grass and other vegetation. Without such competition, and sometimes in spite of it, some of these spread very rapidly. Purple loosestrife (*Lythrum salicaria*), for example, is a European introduction that has ousted native-born plants from many a wet East Coast meadow. Lizard's tail or water dragon (*Saururus cernuus*) is another vigorous colonizer of swamps and shallow water, native from Quebec and Ontario south to Florida and Texas. It is likely to do well in sites where cattails grow. Over heart-shaped leaves up to six inches long rise arched tails of slightly fragrant white flowers. Similar white arched clusters, but shorter, and on taller plants are found on the three-foot Japanese loosestrife or gooseneck, *Lysimachia clethroides*, which spreads rapidly in moist soil.

Those who garden on the banks of creeks and inlets need plants that can tolerate brackish water. Several lovely mallows are native to such sites. Swamp rosemallow, *Hibiscus moscheutos*, bears four-inch white-petalled flowers with a crimson eye on three-to-six-foot bushes. Saltmarsh-mallow, *H.m. palustris*, sometimes called Sea hollyhock, is similar but the flowers are pink. Seashore mallow, *Kosteletzkya virginica*, is a daintier plant with two-inch pale pink flowers. The most impressive, but less hardy than the others, is *Hibiscus coccineus*, which has deeply lobed leaves and bright red flowers four to five inches across. In wet soil it may reach eight feet in height.

All these mallows flower in late summer or early autumn. They are at their best with abundant moisture but also tolerate quite dry soil.

Those who garden, as I do, on tidal creeks, should get acquainted with the sea ox-eye, *Borrichia frutescens*. This has half-inch wide yellow daisies with short, widely spaced ray petals. It is not a "wow" sort of plant, but the fleshy glaucous leaves are attractive and this is one of the few plants that tolerate being two feet or more under salty water when the tide is in.❧

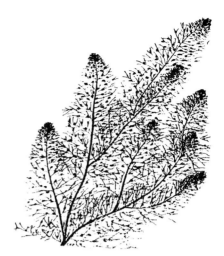

AQUATICS

THE SCOPE OF WATER PLANTS

THOMAS J. DELENDICK

What is an aquatic plant? Simply, it is a plant that grows in water.

If this is so, why do manuals of aquatic plants, like Fassett's and Prescott's (see list of references, p. 78), include such dry-land plants as maples, virburnums, and willows? Because the needs and definitions of an aquarium enthusiast, a home gardener with a small pond, and a vacationer, hiker, or wildlife biologist exploring a lake, bog, or swamp are all different. And most of the manuals that exist deal primarily with the local temperate flora and have the last-mentioned users specifically in mind.

One of the problems in defining aquatic plants centers on the old saw, "Nature mocks men's categories." It is necessary to have a framework in which to organize the body of facts that have accumulated. But it is necessary also to bear in mind that the organization, though convenient, does not fully reflect the complexity of the biological world. In the case of aquatic plants, there is a continuum of "aquatic" habitats from the depths of a lake or stream through swamp, bog, marsh, and seasonally wet shallows and meadows, before one

THOMAS J. DELENDICK, *former Taxonomist at Brooklyn Botanic Garden, has a special interest in aquatic plants and teaches classes on the subject.*

comes up on dry land. And the plants pass variously from one habitat to the next.

For convenience, most water plants will fit into one of five categories. Four of these have an ecological basis; the fifth is distinctly artificial, but by knowing something about a species' natural habits/habitats, it is possible to select plants for a specific water garden or aquarium situation and so increase the chances for success.

Submerged Aquatics

These include those species which actually live underwater for all or nearly all of their natural life cycle. They are rooted in the bottom of the pond/stream/tank, with their stems and leaves submerged, although in some the stems may lengthen to the extent that they "float" beneath the airwater interface. In some submerged aquatics, floating leaves are produced at flowering time.

This group is fairly large and the biology of its members is rather varied. Take, for instance, water-weed (*Elodea canadensis*) (also known as ditch-moss and frog-bit), a North American native which is a common aquarium plant. Although pieces of stem may break off and become free-floating, *Elodea* is basically an underwater plant. The flowers are produced in the axils (the angle between the leaf and the stem) of

A tropical water-lily pool at BBG's Steinhardt Conservatory.

the leaf and, when ready for pollination, are "released." At that time the male flowers are set free from the plant to float on the water surface; the female flowers rise to the surface on elongating pedicels (flower stalks) which, after pollination, coil and draw the spent flower down into the leaf axil. The fruit matures underwater. Eelgrass (*Vallisneria americana*) is closely related to water-weed, although its vegetative appearance is very different.

In contrast, the water starwort (*Callitriche* spp.), so named because when fully developed it produces a rosette of floating leaves, has flowers which develop and are pollinated entirely underwater. The various species of pondweed (*Potamogeton*) are essentially submerged but often produce floating leaves before the aerial inflorescences (flower clusters) appear. Many are interesting and attractive; some have an unfortunate tendency to become weedy.

Quillworts (*Isoetes* spp.) are relatives of the ferns; they look like underwater grasses or sedges but, fernlike, reproduce by means of spores which are produced in sacs at the base of the quill-like "fronds." The fountain moss (*Fontinalis antipyretica*) is one of the few truly aquatic mosses; all members of the genus pass their lives in cold, fast-flowing streams. The cultivated algae are also obligate submergents, including hair-grass (*Nitella* spp.) and stonewort (*Chara* spp.).

Emergent Aquatics

These include those aquatics which are rooted in the substrate (bottom) of their aquatic habitat, but typically produce aerial stems and foliage, although some have only floating leaves. Flowers are produced above the water surface. This is the largest group of aquatics and the most diverse. Delimitation of this category is complicated by the fact that in the wild state some emergents "emerge" by shoot growth above the water surface while the roots and lower stems are in relatively deep water; other emergent species need to have their "feet" wet, but the substrate may be no more than a soggy or marshy habitat with no depth of water to speak of; still others depend for their "emergence" on seasonal fluctuations in the water level of the pond or stream they live in.

Here are found plants like the water lilies (*Nymphaea* spp.) and the sacred lotus (*Nelumbo* spp.) which require a certain minimum depth of water in order to survive the winter (there is a maximum depth, too, below which they will not grow). Both produce floating leaves. The lotus typically produces aerial leaves as the season progresses, but water lilies only when crowded. Water lily-mimics include the floating-hearts and water-snowflakes, members of the genus *Nymphoides*. These resemble *Nymphaea* vegetatively, but their flowers have only five petals and these are somewhat fused at the base—they are in fact more closely related to gentians. *Trapa natans*, one of the water-chestnuts, is a somewhat unique emergent, with highly dissected and threadlike submerged leaves plus a rosette of floating leaves which bear flowers in their axils. They start off life connected to the submerged fruit but with age the connection may be severed and the water-chestnut will float.

Among the "more emergent" emergents are many species of great ecological importance, such as cattails (*Typha* spp.), wild rice (*Zizania aquatica*), and a great many ornamentals. Among the last are the native American golden-club (*Orontium aquaticum*), an aroid with conspicuous yellow flower clusters. Golden-club may be found in water up to a foot deep or growing practically on mud flats. Pickerel-weed (*Pontederia cordata*) has erect clusters of heavenly blue flowers. Water-plantain (*Alisma* spp.), with airy panicles of tiny white flowers, is somewhat reminiscent of baby's-breath. Lizard's-tail (*Saururus cernuus*) has nodding racemes of white flowers. Many species of *Echinodorus*, the sword-plants of aquarists, thrive underwater, but in the wild are essentially emergent and even in cultivation send up aerial leaves and shoots when they reach reproductive maturity.

Many of the most important and ornamental aquarium plants are emergents, such as *Anubias* spp., *Cryptocoryne* spp. (the "crypts"), and *Aponogeton* spp. (including the Madagascar lace plant). They are grown submerged, but since they are attuned to a natural annual cycle of wet/dry or cool/hot seasons in their native habitats they are among the most difficult to keep in cultivation for extended periods.

Floating Aquatics

These include those species which are not rooted in the substrate and are free-floating on or below the surface of the water. Occasionally floaters may be "beached" by wave action or a fall in the water level. Among the flowering plants (which are floaters are the bladderwort (*Utricularia* spp.), one of the carnivorous" plants, which traps and digests water fleas and other minute aquatic animals in its submerged bladders; water-hyacinth (*Eichhornia crassipes*) which has such a bad reputation as a pest in tropical and subtropical waterways; water-lettuce (*Pistia stratiotes*), an aroid and thus a relative of philodendrons and anthuriums; and the duckweeds, *Lemna* spp., *Wolffia* spp., and their relatives—ultra-reduced derivatives of the aroids which include the smallest of all flowering plants.

Opportunistic or Occasional Aquatics

These have a predilection for a moist habitat (lake or river bank) and are subjected to periodic or seasonal changes of water level. Some of these merely tolerate temporary submergence of their roots and stems; others may be found more or less commonly as shallow-water emergents; most can be cultivated in a well-drained situation.

This is where we would put the red and silver maples, viburnums, willows, etc., of the aquatic plant manuals. Bald-cypress (*Taxodium distichum*), which is commonly thought of as a southern swamp tree but which is quite as happy in non-aquatic situations, falls in this category. Several species of Iris and a number of ferns such as ostrich fern (*Matteuccia*), sensitive fern (*Onoclea*), and royal, cinnamon, and interrupted ferns (all of the genus *Osmunda*) are also here, along with most marsh and bog plants (the insectivorous pitcher-plants and sundews).❀

PLANTS FOR PONDS, LAKES AND STREAMS

BILL KESTER

Vaccinium macrocarpon, cranberry

The following information is of interest mainly to persons who are fortunate enough to own or have access to wetlands adjacent to lakes, rivers, or streams, or to people who have constructed, or are contemplating constructing, a pond or lake on their property.

Many of these aquatic plants are a necessity in making sure that the pond or lake will remain clear, healthy, and full of living creatures. Through the process of photosynthesis, living plants are able to turn carbon dioxide in the water and the air into carbohydrates for their own use by the action of the sunlight on its chlorophyll. Therefore, they purify the water, release vitally needed oxygen into the air and water, provide shade from the sun's rays in warm weather, and bind the bottom soils. It is very seldom that a pond or lake will remain muddy if it contains plants.

Plants also provide excellent cover for young fish and waterfowl. Insects, crustaceans, plankton, and other organisms and animal life abound and reproduce rapidly on and among these plants, thus providing food for fish, waterfowl, and some mammals. Many of these plants are valuable sources of food in the form of seeds, nutlets, tubers, fruits, roots, and foliage that is needed for waterfowl, upland birds, and mammals. Following is a list of some of the plants you can plant in and around your ponds, lakes, or wetlands, with a brief description of how, where, and when to plant and of their value to wildlife and the environment.

Sweet flag (*Acorus calamus*). Plant in the same conditions as iris. Its flower is unusual—it grows from the side of one of its leaf stalks and the resulting seed head resembles a cattail head. The leaves are lemony and the roots have a sweet spicy aromatic fragrance.

Swamp milkweed (*Asclepias incarnata*). Pretty perennial with rose-purple flowers followed by long narrow seed pods that split open like the upland milkweed. Plant any time in damp soil. Grows to a height of about 3 feet.

Sedge (*Carex* spp.). Prefers shallow ponds, sloughs, or marshes. It has a three-sided stem, and varies in height from 18 inches to 3 feet. It provides a dense root system for binding the soil. It has a pretty ornamental seed head, but

Pontederia cordata

not much food value. Perennial; plant any time of the year.

Spike rush (*Eleocharis acicularis*). Perennial; plant any time of year. Grows best in shallow water, muddy flats, swales, and marshes, in ponds, lakes, or streams throughout the United States. Small round-stemmed plant growing from 8 to 18 inches high.

Joe-Pye weed (*Eupatorium*). Perennial wetland flower with purplish flowers which grow to a height of 3 to 4 feet. The rootstock can be planted any time in damp soil.

Blue and yellow water irises (*Iris germanica*). Prefer damp soil or shallow water, but will tolerate soil that later dries out. Plant on borders of ponds, lakes, streams, or marshy areas. Have beautiful blue or yellow flowers and lancelike leaves. Most are ornamental perennials and can be planted any time.

Watercress (*Nasturtium officinale*). Prefers spring-fed brooks and ponds. Excellent food for humans and waterfowl. As the seed is very fine, almost like pepper, we suggest mixing with dry sand when planting. An annual, but reseeds itself.

American lotus (*Nelumbo lutea*). Prefers shallow-water bays and sluggish streams or lakes. Indians used the seeds and tubers for food. A perennial and ornamental. (See p. 19.)

Wild water lily or **Spatterdock** (*Nuphar advena*). Grows in shallow protected areas

W. A. (BILL) KESTER, *Vice President, Kester's Wild Game Food Nurseries, Inc., Omro, Wisconsin, has written many articles and has been in the business for over 40 years.*

of ponds, lakes, or streams. Has a large rootstock, 4 to 6 inches in diameter. This is a perennial and can be planted any time. Ornamental.

Magnolia water lily (*Nymphaea tuberosa*). Grows best in shallow water 1 to 2-feet-deep in ponds, lakes and in the sheltered bays of streams. The lily has a parent rootstock that resembles a banana with small tubers (about 3/4 inch in diameter and 3 to 4 inches in length) fastened to it. If you want flowers the first year, the large parent rootstock should be planted because the small tuber may not bloom for several years. Provides excellent cover for fish, especially bass, as they wait for a frog to jump off the lily pad. Available in white and many colors and all are perennials.

Reed or Cane (*Phragmites* spp.). Stalks have hollow sections similar to a cane fishing pole. It grows up to 8 feet and provides shelter for all wildlife. Perennial; plant any time of the year in wet soils along ponds, lakes, streams, or marshes.

Nodding smartweed (*Polygonum punctatum*). Plant root sections at any time of the year in damp soil, and in water up to 10 inches deep. Provides some cover for wildlife, but usually matures to about two feet high. Produces some small round flat black seeds that waterfowl and upland game birds eat. It produces an amazing thick network of running ropelike roots.

These roots are about the thickness of a pencil and I have seen them 20 to 30 feet long—very good for erosion control. Survives drought as well as periodic flooding after it becomes established.

Pickerel weed (*Pontederia cordata*). Besides being a good cover plant for fish, this beautiful ornamental has a spike of bright blue flowers and heart-shaped leaves. It is a perennial. Plant in water 1 or 2 feet deep at any time of the year. Its seeds are also eaten by waterfowl. It can be planted in ponds or lakes.

Sago pondweed (*Potamogeton pectinatus*). Plant in water 1 to 3 feet deep from early spring through summer, or later in the southern states, as long as you have about 100 days for it to mature. It grows in almost any waters, including small ponds, throughout the United States, but not in strong salty waters. It produces tubers in the soil, as well as setting seed, and both are excellent food for waterfowl. The foliage provides cover for fish and purifies and clarifies the water. As these tubers float they must be weighted in some manner to keep them at the bottom of the pond or lake so they can take root.

Arrowhead, Wapato or **duck potato** (*Sagittaria latifolia*). Plant in spring and summer on wet mud flats and in water up to 18 inches deep; requires about 120 days of growing weather. Arrowhead will

58

grow in small ponds, lakes, or streams. However, in large lakes it needs protection from wave action. Plant in sheltered bays or coves, or where there are bulrushes or reeds. They grow well in most inland waters except those tainted with strong lime, alkali, or salt. Arrowhead is excellent for planting as a bed for filtering polluted waters, as it is one of the heaviest feeders of rich nutrients. The richer, more fertile the soil, the larger the plant will grow. In high nutrient areas it will produce 2- or 3-inch tubers similar to domestic potato; the size of the tuber in non-fertile waters will range from a marble to golf ball size. The color of the tubers will vary from white to cream, red, blue, or purple. Because of its high starch content, this tuber is one of the best muskrat foods. The tubers and crisp parts of the plant are valuable waterfowl food. The large tubers were a staple food for the Indians who showed the early settlers how to use them. The early Chinese immigrants used the tubers for starch in their laundries and also considered them a very healthy table vegetable. The leaf is shaped like an arrow and the plant has a white blossom.

Deep-water duck potato (*Sagittaria rigida*). Plant in water 1 to 2 feet deep in spring and summer; requires 120 days for maturing. Not suited for small ponds as it prefers moving or slow flowing streams, sloughs, large ponds, or lakes. The leaves are the shape of a chicken-wing feather and the plant produces small yellow tubers which are another favorite food of waterfowl.

Hard-stem bulrush (*Scirpus acutus*) and Soft-stem bulrush (*S. validus*). Plant at any time of the year in wet soils, and in water up to 18 inches deep. Foliage is a hollow tube-like stem that grows 3 to 5 feet tall, tapered on the end. It produces seed that is eaten by waterfowl, and muskrats will feed on some of the roots and also use the foliage for house building. When growing some distance out from the shoreline, it provides a buffer zone that breaks the wave action. This deters shoreline erosion, quiets the waters, and allows other food-producing aquatics such as wild celery, sago pondweed, deep-water duck potato and arrowhead to grow. Provides shelter for waterfowl and fish.

Three-square rush (*Scirpus fluviatilis*). Plant at any time of year on damp soil, and in water up to 12 inches deep. It produces a series of hard, stonelike tubers in the soil which are connected together with a runner or rhizome that when mature is about the size and strength of bailing wire. This network of hard tubers and wirelike runners form a massive root structure that binds the soil together to prevent erosion. It grows 4 to 6 feet tall on a strong three-cornered stem.

Bur reed (*Sparganium eurycarpum*). Plant any time of the year in damp soil and in water up to 10 inches deep. It grows approximately three feet high with leaves that resemble cattail. Has an ornamental seed head about golf ball size with diamond-shaped seeds that are eaten to some extent by waterfowl and upland game birds. Its roots are a favorite food of muskrats and the foliage is used by them to build their houses. Do not let the name bur reed confuse you because it does not have a bur that sticks to clothing or animal hair. In a small pond plant a couple of bur reed with a few arrowhead in the same pot. This makes a pretty ornamental combination.

Cord grass (*Spartina alterniflora, S. pectinata*). Perennial; can be planted at any time of the year. Prefers shallow water in ponds, lakes, streams, or marshy areas subject to flooding, but will survive dry periods. *S. alterniflora* grows best in salt marshes whereas *S. pectinata* is widespread throughout the United States in fresh and salt water. Cord grass is an important soil binder along the water's edge and provides cover and some food for waterfowl and muskrats. Grows 4- to 6-feet-tall and is very attractive with its waving plume or seed head.

Iris pseudacorus

Photo by Elvin McDonald

Cattail (*Typha latifolia, T. augustifolia*). For best results plant in damp soil or water up to 10 inches deep, although they will grow in deeper water. Rootstocks can be planted at any time of the year. Provide excellent cover for waterfowl, upland game birds, song birds, and other wildlife. The rootstocks are an excellent food for muskrats and its foliage is used for building their houses.

Wild celery (*Vallisneria spiralis*). The same cultural information as above, except that it will not grow in stagnant or small landlocked ponds. It requires fresh moving water, either flowing water or water moved back and forth by the wind.

Wild rice (*Zizania aquatica*). Plant seed in fall or spring in water 6 to 18 inches deep in coves or bays where it is sheltered from strong waves. Wild rice will not grow in stagnant, strongly alkaline, limey, or salt water. Needs movement or changing of water by wind action or a slow-moving stream. Ripe seed can be thrown into the water and it will sink to the bottom. It reseeds each year. Wild rice is an excellent food for waterfowl, and muskrats will eat or cut off the young stalks for food for themselves and their young. This was one of the staple foods for the Indians.

Many of the plants listed will grow in different depths of water or in other soil conditions. I have merely noted those conditions that will give the best results. Also remember, any pond, lake, or wetland should be managed the same as a farm or a garden. Many plants may take over a pond or wetland unless controlled. This is especially true of the non-food-producing plants which are vigorous competitors. ❀

BELOW IS A PICTORIAL VIEW OF A SUGGESTED PLANTING, SHOWING WHERE TO PLANT VARIOUS AQUATIC PLANTS.

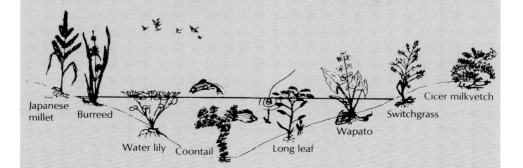

Japanese millet Burreed Water lily Coontail Long leaf Wapato Switchgrass Cicer milkvetch

Plant in Damp to Dry Soils
Switchgrass
Reed canary grass
False bittersweet
Jerusalem artichoke

Plant in Water 1-8 inches deep
Arrowhead
Wild rice
Tame rice
Bulrush
Pickerel weed

Plant in Water 4-6 inches deep
American lotus

Plant in Water 1-2 feet deep
Deep-water duck potato
Water lilies

Plant in Water 1-6 feet deep
Coontail
Elodea
Naiad
Muskgrass
Ducksmeat

Plant in Damp to Muddy Soils
Blue water iris
Yellow water iris
Sweet flag
Japanese millet
Browntop millet
Lowland smartweed
Millet
Sesbania
Alali bulrush

Plant in Water 1-10 inches
Bur reed
Nodding smartweed
Three-square rush
Cattail
Wampee duck corn
Watercress

Plant in Water 1-3 feet deep
Sago pondweed
Wild celery
Long-leaf pondweed
Redhead grass

Plant in Dry Soils of Ditch Banks Surrounding Soils
(soil to be worked up and planted)
Cicer milkvetch
Birdsfoot trefoil
Crownvetch
Wild white clover
Coniferous trees
Mixed game bird seed
Deer plot mix seed
Pearl millet
Proso millet
Milo
Tioga deer tongue
Small burnet
Hegari
Dove proso millet
Duckwheat
Lespedeza
Kester's peas
Field peas
Winter wheat
Buckwheat
Perennial grain
Lathco flat pea
Aeschynomene

Bog Plants of the Northeast

Jacqueline Fazio

The process that transforms open ponds or wet areas into a spongy, seemingly solid mats can take thousands of years to complete. A bog is formed by an accumulation of plant debris on a foundation of intertwining roots from trees and shrubs. As the wet area fills in, the water beneath stagnates and becomes oxygen starved, decomposition slows, and nutrients become scare. The result is a very acidic environment that suits specific types of plants.

Although bogs are not the most common wetlands in the northeast, they are of special interest to naturalists, offering a unique assortment of flora. Bogs develop in a variety of habitats, from the sandy coastal plains of New Jersey, Long Island, and Cape Cod to the cooler woodlands of northern New England.

Trees

In these colder regions of New England, black spruce (*Picea mariana*) and larch or tamarack (*Larix laricina*) are the predominant conifers initiating bog development. The black spruce is the more invasive of the

JACQUELINE FAZIO, *Curator of the Local Flora Section, Brooklyn Botanic Garden, has studied native plants and their environments for over five years.*

two trees, sometimes forming pure stands. This spruce is a source for pulpwood and is often logged. The larch, although present in these boglands, does not find this environment as favorable and rarely reaches its maximum height in this habitat. Its range extends further south into northern Connecticut. As cooler weather approaches in New England, larches show their true colors. The needles of these deciduous conifers turn bright orange-yellow, then drop. White cedar (*Chamaecyparis thyoides*) grows in the bogs of southern New England and the coastal plains areas. It forms the purest stands of any North American tree. The wood is light in weight and decay-resistant, and consequently these stands are sometimes decimated by lumbering.

Shrubs

The acid conditions that exist in bogs provide an excellent habitat for shrubs of the Heath Family (*Ericaceae*). They grow on the edges of the bog and sometimes form colonies on the soggy surface. Some of the most commonly found members of this family include leatherleaf (*Chamaedaphne calyculata*), a semievergreen shrub with white flowers which blooms in April/June, and Labrador tea (*Ledum groenlandicum*), a northern bog shrub with dark green leaves with fuzzy brown undersides and white flowers that appear on terminal clusters in May/June. The fragrant leaves of Labrador tea were brewed as a substitute for tea during colonial times. Rhodora (*Rhododendron canadense*) is a low shrub with slightly pubescent leaves. Its azalealike magenta flowers appear in May before the leaves. Sweet pepperbush (*Clethra alnifolia*) has fragrant white flowers in July/August. Cranberry (*Vaccinium macrocarpon* and *V. oxycoccos*) is a creeping shrub with small leaves. The flowers are pink and appear in June/July. The fruit is a bright red berry maturing in October. It is commercially cultivated for its berries in parts of New Jersey and Cape Cod. Other shrubs of interest include bog-laurel (*Kalmia polifolia*), sheep-laurel (*K. angustifolia*), bog-rosemary (*Andromeda glaucophylla*), poison sumac (*Rhus vernix*), and sweet gale (*Myrica gale*) which is a member of the Myricaceae, the bayberry family.

ering on the bog. Its ability to absorb water, up to ten times its weight, contributes to keeping the surface of the bog cool and moist. Peat moss is decayed sphagnum moss.

Insectivorous plants also grow in bogs. Plants such as the thread-leaved and round-leaved sundew (*Drosera filiformis* and *D. rotundifolia*) grow here as does the only northern species of pitcher plant (*Sarracenia purpurea*). Bladderwort (*Utricularia* spp.) is a genus of about two hundred species of which approximately five are found in bogs in this area.

Terrestrial orchids have adapted to the nutrient-poor habitat of bogs by forming a symbiotic relationship with mycorrhiza (soil fungi). These mycorrhiza penetrate the roots of the orchids, delivering nutrients from the soil and, it is believed, receiving complex organic compounds in return. The difficulty in getting this fungus established accounts for the problems in transplanting these orchids. The most common orchid genus in southern New England is the fringed orchid (*Habenaria* spp.). Other orchids include rose pogonia (*Pogonia ophioglossoides*), swamp pink (*Arethusa bulbosa*), and grass pink (*Calopogon tuberosus*). All have pink flowers and all bloom from May to August. Showy lady's slipper

Herbaceous Plants and Ferns

There is an unusual variety of herbaceous plants existing on the bog surface. Sphagnum moss (*Sphagnum* sp.), a bryophyte, grows prolifically in this environment. It forms a soft green cov-

(*Cypripedium reginae*) and pink lady's slip-per (*C. acaule*) are occasionally found in the cooler northern bogs of New England.

There are other assorted herbaceous plants found in bogs. Cotton grass (*Eriophorum virginicum*), a member of the Sedge Family (*Cyperaceae*), forms tussocks on the surface of open bogs. The bog - hyacinth (*Helonias bullata*) and bog-aspho-del (*Narthecium americanum*) are both found in the southern part of the north-east, while the bog-bean (*Menyanthes trifoli-ata*) grows in the cooler bogs of the north-ern northeast.

Mosses and ferns also grow in boggy environments. Fox-tail clubmoss (*Lycopodium alopecuroides*) and Carolina clubmoss (*L. carolinianum*) are found in the southerly coastal plains area. The regal fern (*Osmunda regalis*) and cinnamon fern (*O. cinnamomea*) thrive throughout the boglands of the entire northeast. The rare curly-grass fern (*Schizaea pusilla*) is found only in bogs of southern New Jersey. Its miniature size makes it difficult to find even where it is abundant.

Making Your Own Bog

A bog can be created in a backyard. It requires a fair amount of work, however. Dig an area three feet in depth of a size and shape to suit your garden. Line the inside of the hole with concrete, heavy plastic, or tile. Fill the area as follows:

Photo by Peter K. Nelson

Showy lady's slipper.

3 ft.	18"	Sphagnum peat moss
	12"	Builder's sand
	6"	Coarse gravel

It is important that the roots of the plants have constant moisture. The cor-rect soil pH is also crucial for these plants. A pH between 3.5 (very acid) and 5 (moderately acid) is desirable. To increase (sweeten) the pH of the soil add lime; to decrease (acidify) add alu-minum sulfate at the appropriate rate. pH test kits and the above supplies should be available at local garden cen-

Iris pseudacorus *along BBG's stream.*

Lobelia cardinalis, *cardinal flower.*

ters with directions on their use. Flood the area several times until the peat moss is soggy and saturated, then check the pH. Once the pH is correct, start planting.

A large number of bog plants are protected by law. If you find a source for these plants, please make certain that they are reliable growers and not collecting plants from the wild.❀

65

TROPICAL AND TEMPERATE WATER PLANTS FOR THE HOME AQUARIUM

MICHAEL RAMIREZ

Growing aquatic and semi-aquatic plants in the home is becoming increasingly popular. A suitable selection of water plants tastefully planted in an aquarium under grow lights with decorative rocks and even driftwood can be very attractive. The beauty of water plants prospering in their aquatic environment presents an appealing picture.

Aquariums can be purchased in many shapes and sizes. A convenient size is a twenty-gallon rectangular tank. Smaller aquariums of 5, 10, and 15 gallons are also available.

Growing Medium

A good planting medium is a mixture of one part (by volume) clay soil to three parts of unwashed fine-textured yellow builder's sand. Moisten the mixture and place on the bottom of the aquarium. The soil mix can be contoured, sloping from the back toward the front. A slope of four to two inches in depth is desirable. The sloping bottom can be held in place by terracing with non-toxic rocks, driftwood, or petrified wood, available at most tropical fish dealers. When using the mixture of clay and sand, top it off with a thin layer of No. 1 aquarium or bird gravel to prevent clouding of the water when the aquarium is being filled.

When the soil mixture is in place, cover with a towel or several layers of newspaper. Then fill slowly with tap water to a depth of one-third to one-half of the height of your aquarium. This will facilitate planting without getting wet. Use a water conditioner to remove chlorine or simply allow the water to stand twenty-four hours before planting. When filling your aquarium, condition or age the water in the same manner.

Light

Strong light is essential for the proper growth of aquatic plants. I have used a total of 90 watts of cool-white fluorescent tubes for a 55-gallon aquarium. Incidental natural light from a nearby window with morning sun will contribute the full spectrum of light that the plants need. Experiment with the amount of light necessary for your aquarium. Twelve hours of light daily will keep the tropical water plants growing and, in some instances, prevent water plants from the temperate regions from becoming dormant, or losing their leaves. Newly planted aquariums are susceptible to growth of algae. If the water becomes green or cloudy or a film of algae begins to grow on the plants and rocks, cut down the amount of light.

Accessories

Electric heaters and thermometers are necessary for aquariums containing tropical water plants. The optimum growing temperature is 75-80 degrees F. A lower autumn and winter night temperature of 70 degrees is beneficial.

A combination thermostat-heater of 250 watts is adequate for an aquarium of 50-55 gallons. Consult a tropical fish dealer for the correct wattages for other sizes. An accurate thermometer is also necessary to check the heater's temperature settings.

A cold water or unheated aquarium will depend on room temperature for its heat. In the winter, a night temperature of 50-60 degrees is preferable for plants from the temperate regions.

Filters

A filter serves several purposes. It will filter out small particles of matter and keep the water clear. The water movement will also ensure a uniform temperature throughout the aquarium. A further benefit is the aeration by agitation. A small power filter for aquariums of thirty gallons and up is adequate. For a smaller aquarium, use a small bubble-up inside or outside the filter. The under-gravel filters do not seem to work as well.

Plants for Heated Aquariums

In selecting plants for heated aquariums, the water gardener can choose from three categories; stem or branch plants, single plants with crowns, or floating plants. Stem plants include *Hygrophila* spp., *Rotala* spp., and some *Myriophyllum* spp., all of which are sold in bunches. Remove the lead weights and rubber bands and make fresh cuttings of 6 to 8 inches. Strip off the bottom leaves to expose two or three nodes and insert the stem into the sand. Plant these tall-growing plants in groups in the back and corners of aquariums.

Crown plants, such as *Echinodorus* spp. and varieties known collectively as sword plants, have both tall-and shorter-growing members. The tall-growing, narrow-leaved sword (*E. amazonicus)* makes a splendid centerpiece, as does the broad-leaved sword (*E. bleheri*). Another suitable candidate for this purpose is the handsome, ruffled, broad-leaved sword (*E. leopoldina*) which has long, undulating leaves. For the front of the aquarium, pygmy chain-sword (*E. tenellus*) is the smallest of the genus and grows in a rosette with runners.

Other plants suitable for use a focal points are the larger species of *Anubias* and *Aponogeton*. *Vallisneria* spp. and varieties are thoroughly aquatic in habit and appearance. They grow rapidly and spread by runners. Confine by cutting back some of the runners. V. *spiralis* and V. *americana* are taller plants suitable for the background and corners of aquarium. There are also smaller varieties with lovely twisted leaves.

Cryptocoryne is a large genus of marsh and aquatic plants. Many can live and prosper permanently under water. A few that are notable are the small C. *willisii*, C. *affinis*, C. *beckettii*, C. *haerteliana*, and C. *petchii*. All have colorful leaves in shades of copper, red, and brown tones and can be used for contrast. They spread slowly by underground runners and in time make lovely ground covers. C. *balansae*, C. *bullosa*, and C. *usteriana* are light-loving and have long, wide strap-shaped leaves that are wonderfully crinkled.

Aquatic ferns, such as *Ceratopteris* spp., *Microsorium* spp., and *Bolbitis* spp., are valuable plants to grow in the aquarium. Java fern (*Microsorium*) grows best when its lateral rhizome is attached to a stone or a piece of weighted driftwood. Treat *Bolbitis* spp. in the same way. Plant water fern (*Ceratopteris* spp.) in the same manner as the aquatic plants previously described.

Floating plants include *Salvinia* spp., *Lemna* spp. (duckweed), dwarf water lilies, *Azolla* spp., and some varieties of *Ceratopteris*. They are not suitable for aquariums because they will cast shade on the bottom-growing plants. However, if their spread is restricted by frequent thinning, they will not cause problems.

Plants for Unheated Aquariums

Bunches of plants such as *Elodea*, *Myriophyllum, Ludwigia, Cabomba*, and *Ceratophyllum* can be used. *Aponogeton* species will do very well, since they will require a cooler resting period in the winter months. Among them is *Aponogeton fenestralis*, the famous Madagascar lace plant. Species of *Sagittaria* are also suitable.

The list of plants described above is not exhaustive; dealers and growers specializing in aquatic plants can suggest many more. Do not use traditional house plants such as *Dracaena, Maranta,* or *Fittonia* which are often sold as aquatics, because they will not survive underwater. Experiment to find out what performs best in your aquarium environment and suits your taste.✿

CULTIVATING AN INDOOR MARSH

JOSEPH S. LEVINE

A break in the fog reveals a scene of unusual beauty. Water is everywhere; it permeates the soil, hangs in the saturated atmosphere, collects in the centers of epiphytic bromeliads, and glistens in droplets on delicately colored flowers. An Asian newt stalks ponderously along submerged leaves and branches, pausing periodically to catch a breath at the surface of the water. The newt startles a killifish who dashes out of his hiding place in a thicket of aquatic vegetation and dives into a small underwater cave. Around this new refuge, amphibious mosses and ferns make the transition from aquatic to terrestrial life, climbing onto the rocks at the base of a trickling waterfall. Cascading down the rocks along with the water are several species of *Selaginella* and a trailing *Peperomia*, whose adventitious roots stretch toward the duckweed floating on the water surface below.

JOSEPH S. LEVINE, *Assistant Professor of Biology at Boston College is currently a research associate at Harvard's Museum of Comparative Zoology and the Marine Biological Laboratory in Woods Hole. He writes textbooks and popular volumes on biology and marine ecology; advisor on television series* Nova *and* Living Wild.

The preceding passage might be based on a trip to an Old-World rain forest, but is actually a description of a scene created within the confines of a converted 55-gallon fish tank. Finding an accurate label for this type of miniature environment is significantly more difficult than building one. It is obviously not an aquarium, but the standard term *terrarium* doesn't quite fit either. With so much water around, there is precious little terra firma in evidence. A "swamparium" perhaps? The connotation is less than pleasing. Once again a retreat into Latin saves the day for the horticulturist, as we resurrect the term *paludarium* from its post-Victorian fall from grace. According to *Webster's Seventh Collegiate Dictionary*, the adjective *paludal* refers or relates to marshes or fens, which are in turn defined as "low land covered wholly or partly with water." In their book *Aquarium Plants*, Ratraj and Horeman define paludariums as "containers, usually tanks, in which a marsh-like environment is maintained; tanks suitable for amphibious plants and animals."

The Growth Medium

Experienced indoor botanists may be wondering about the water-saturated environment under discussion. Usually the first—the most important—lesson learned by beginning gardeners is to take extreme caution not to overwater plants in containers that lack drainage holes. If heavy soil remains saturated for long, water replaces air in the interstices of the medium. If the situation is not remedied, bacterial activity adds toxic metabolic by-products to the soil and the pH drops precipitously. When soil "goes sour" in this fashion, further root growth is inhibited—even in species that don't mind wet feet—and the plants usually die.

Proper selection of a planting medium helps avoid problems of this type in the paludarium. A soilless mixture composed of two parts sphagnum peat moss, one part vermiculite, one part coarse perlite, one part aquarium-grade activated charcoal, and one tablespoon of ground limestone per gallon of mix is just right for closed-container planting. The major components of the medium give it a light and airy texture, while the charcoal and limestone keep the pH within tolerable limits for long periods of time. The use of sterilized components minimizes the introduction of pathogenic soil microorganisms and insects, while the absence of nutrients for plant growth allows the grower a greater degree of control over plant growth. If rampant growth is desired, the mix can be moistened with a dilute balanced fertilizer solution at planting time. Alternatively, slow-release fertilizer pellets can be added to the medium. Local variations in the nature of the planting medium can be arranged to suit the needs of particular plants. Pockets of pure, live sphagnum moss provide the proper conditions for many carnivorous plants, which strongly resent the addition of any chemical fertilizer in the vicinity of their roots. Large flat rocks and fungicide-soaked pieces of tree bark can be used to create raised areas for species that prefer slightly less water-logged conditions.

Light

Once the medium has been selected, the grower must provide sufficient light to ensure proper plant growth. Low light levels in terrariums are the usual cause of weak, leggy growth, even in ostensibly shade-loving species.

If your paludarium is to be left uncovered, it can be placed near a window to utilize available sunlight. The high humidity required by a number of exotic paludarium species, however, necessitates that tight-fitting covers be employed to maintain a saturated atmosphere. Closed containers of this type should never be placed in direct sunlight, as the resultant rapid overheating will quickly cook the contents. The best solution to the lighting problem in such cases is the provision of 14 to 16 hours of fluorescent light daily. A minimum of two fluorescent tubes the length of the chosen container is recommended. A paludarium in a 10- or 15-gallon fish tank can get by on two 15- or 20-watt bulbs, but a 55-gallon aquarium should be provided with at least a pair of 40-watt tubes. When choosing containers to be illuminated in this manner, keep in mind that light intensity drops off roughly as the square of the distance between the bulbs and the leaves of the plants. Long, low containers generally allow better illumination than short, high ones.

Planning

The actual planning and planting of a paludarium can be as simple or as elaborate as you desire. The design of your personal paludarium is limited only by your imagination and ingenuity. The instructions and suggestions that follow are meant only as guidelines to spark your own creativity.

A primary consideration in your design, of course, is the relative area you wish to devote to dry land and water spaces within your container. I generally disavow any bias and split up the terrain roughly 50-50, although never in a symmetrical manner. The actual division between land and water spaces is made with pieces of one-eighth-inch-thick glass cut into strips several inches wide (the exact width depending on the desired depth of the water area) and varying lengths. These

strips are laid out end to end in any pleasing nonsymmetrical path across the bottom of the tank, separating an aquatic area in the front from a terrestrial one in the rear. Once the desired position of the strips has been determined, they are glued into position on the bottom and sealed to each other and to the sides of the tank using clear plastic aquarium sealant. The sealant must be allowed to cure for a full 24 hours, after which the aquatic area should be filled with water to test all internal seams for leaks. If tropical aquatic plants and animals are part of your master plan—as well they should be—you will need to install a submersible thermostatically controlled water heater in the aquatic section. Estimate the amount of water held in the aquatic compartment, and, allowing 5 watts per gallon, purchase the appropriate size heater. For such shallow-water setups, the completely submersible type of heaters are best; these are positioned horizontally and can be hidden behind aquatic vegetation.

Now is the time to consider the incorporation of a waterfall into your design. Whether you choose to create a gently trickling mountain spring or a rushing cataract, the charm of moving water will add an entirely unexpected dimension to your ecosystem in miniature. The type of pump you choose to lift the water will depend upon the amount of water you want it to move; miniature submersible pumps are available from water-garden companies. Once you have the chosen pump in hand, hook it up in a sink or bathtub to get a firsthand idea of the volume of water it will pump to the height you desire through the tubing size you wish to use. With a clear mental picture of this flow in mind, you are ready to

design the waterfall itself.

In my paludarium the waterfall is of the striking type and is situated completely in the aquatic compartment. Thus, the submersible pump is simply hidden in a bunch of underwater moss, and a tube is run to the top of a carefully arranged group of rocks from where the water is allowed to drip and splash freely into the "river" below. With this design, I simply arranged the rocks as I liked and glued them together with clear plastic aquarium sealer. Wherever I wanted water to flow along an area where two rocks met, I merely sealed the seam between them with cement and, where necessary, glued a few pebbles along the way to hide any artificial-looking gaps. If you prefer a waterfall that falls across the entire length of your terrestrial area before it reaches the bottom, you can construct a channel for it out of instant cement mix. In either case, time and care should be taken to arrange rocks and other natural objects to eliminate all hints of artifice. Naturally, a little advance planning will help you in this regard. Leisurely summer strolls along beaches and through woods provided me with assorted river stones, gravel, and

unusual pieces of driftwood and bark, all of which were stored away to be sorted over at paludarium planting time. Most natural objects of this type quickly become substrates for mosses and creeping ferns in paludariums, making the scene look unexpectedly realistic.

Once either the waterfall or other landscaped centerpiece has been arranged, it is time to collect the plants and get to work on the horticultural part of the endeavor.

Suitable Plants

What kind of plant species can be utilized in this kind of artificial environment? Depending on your preferences and skill, you can include a number of unusual species that will thrive in a very wet environment.

Aquatic mosses and ferns are perfect paludarium specimens. If they are obtained in their aquatic growth forms and placed underwater, they will grow submerged for indeterminate periods of time and then suddenly begin to climb out onto wet rocks or damp pieces of wood. In the process, their appearance will change.

73

Species of *Vesicularia*, or Java moss, and *Marsilea*, or water clover—which is actually a fern and not a clover at all—are particularly attractive. Other ferns that produce larger fronds can also make a water-to-air transition in a humid paludarium, but instead of creeping out, they suddenly throw out aerial fronds from just beneath the water's surface. Java ferns (*Polypodium pteropus*) produce aerial fronds that differ little in appearance from their submerged ones, but the water sprites (*Ceratopteris* spp.) give rise to above-water fronds bearing little or no resemblance to the aquatic form.

Many other plants commonly cultivated in aquariums will reveal their true amphibious dispositions if given the opportunity to grow in a paludarium. Species of *Rotala*, *Ludwigia*, *Alternanthera*, and many other so-called bunch plants sold in pet stores can be placed underwater and allowed to continue tip growth out into the air, where they will often flower. Many of the various Amazon sword plants (*Echinodorus* spp.) will grow contentedly as aquatics in shallow water for a time, and then suddenly begin to produce first floating and then emergent leaves. The genus *Cryptocoryne* contains many beautiful small-growing species that are generally rather difficult to cultivate totally submerged. If planted with their roots in soggy soil and their leaves in the saturated atmosphere of the paludarium, however, they grow remarkably well, often flowering and reproducing vegetatively the same time.

An earlier HORTICULTURE article on aquarium plants (June 1979) described species native to amphibious habitats along tropical rivers. Because of widely fluctuating water levels in these areas, the native plants have been forced to adapt themselves to alternate submersion and emersion on a seasonal basis. Although they need to function underwater for long periods of time, these plants are prevented from becoming totally aquatic by periodic exposure to air. In fact, since most of their time is spent in a condition midway between total submersion and total emersion, the majority of these species grow and flower best with their leaves in air and their roots in waterlogged soil. These are paludarium plants par excellence.

Straddling the air-water interface are assorted species of *Selaginella*—a paludarium keeper's delight. Resembling a cross between a large moss and a small fern, *Selaginella* species revel in the wet, warm, humid paludarium environment, growing densely and attractively if provided with good fluorescent light. If placed at a land-water junction, they will grow in both directions, sending runners along the surface of the soil and for long distances underwater. They are ideal for growing over rocks and bark and will eventually hide your waterfall if you are not ruthless in trimming them back. Several *Selaginella* species are peculiarly slow about becoming established in a new environment; they occasionally take several weeks to settle in. Once they have established themselves, though, stand back! *Selaginella kraussiana* is the most commonly encountered species, with two attractive cultivars: the yellowtipped *S. kraussiana* 'Aurea' and the dwarf, emerald-green *S. kraussiana* 'Brownii'. Other species are usually available only from mail-order plant specialists but are certainly worth hunting for. Forms and colors vary from the creeping, iridescent blue-green *S.*

uncinata to the upright, arborescent, white-variegated *S. martensii* forma *albolineata*, and the spreading, fanlike *S. pallescens*.

Houseplant Prospects

Several familiar houseplants can also serve as temporary members of small paludariums or permanent parts of larger ones. Horticultural varieties of Chinese evergreen (*Aglaonema modestum*) and seedling palms like *Chamaedorea elegans* are good examples of old favorites with hidden amphibious sides to their personalities. Both grow well with wet feet, and their height and leaf structures make them valuable as "trees" in your miniature landscape. The only problem is that both of these plants will probably grow so well in the paludarium that they will outgrow their allotted space in a year or so. Palms will have to be removed at this time, but *Aglaonema* species can simply be cut back and the tip cuttings planted.

Moving just above the waterline, we come to the preferred microhabitat of a number of exquisite flowering and foliage plants belonging to the Genseriaceae Family. Members of the genus *Gesneria* are especially suitable for paludarium culture. They remain relatively compact, flower extremely well under fluorescent lights, and like to be kept constantly moist. Both *G. cuneifolia*, with its narrow green leaves and tubular, firecracker-red flowers, and *G. humilis*, with its smaller habit and bright yellow flowers, add splashes of color to the scene with their periodic blooms.

Although carnivorous plants are ideal subjects for wet, humid places, most of them require prodigious amounts of light in order to grow compactly and acquire their full color. If your paludarium is of a long, low configuration, you can experiment with several species of *Drosera* (sundews), *Utricularia* (bladderworts), and, of course, the famous *Dionaea*, the Venus flytrap. These carnivores prefer pockets of live sphagnum and as intense a dosage of fluorescent light as you can arrange to give them. Somewhat less demanding in light requirements and equally fascinating in appearance are several of the smaller species of *Nepenthes*, exotic tropical pitcher plants that are semiepiphytic but must never be allowed to dry out.

Several rare and extremely beautiful begonias like *Begonia versicolor* and its hybrids, as well as the rare *Symbegonia* species from Australia, add colorful foliage to the scene. Keep your eyes open in the not-too-distant future for the true miniature rex begonias currently being hybridized. Today's rex begonias all grow far too large for paludarium culture, but these true miniatures—with full-grown leaves no larger than a quarter—will surely take the country by storm when they are released in a few years. Other difficult-to-find gems include a few tiny *Calathea* species like *Calathea micans* and *C. undulata* and a few truly miniature ferns. Beware of most "dwarf" ferns and begonias that are widely available; while normally diminutive, they will usually triple their size under the ideal conditions of a paludarium.✺

Reprinted courtesy of *Horticulture, The Magazine of American Gardening*, 755 Boylston St., Boston, MA 02116. Copyright (C) *1980*, Horticulture Associates.

GEORGE H. PRING

WATER LILY HYBRIDIST

DENI SEIBERT (ISABELLE PRING)

Nymphaea 'Mrs. George H. Pring'

Photo by Bob Scherer

Pistia stratiotes

Photo by Elvin McDonald

Growing up with a father who was the world's expert on tropical lilies made life a carousel of enchantment. George Harry Ethelbert Pring (he took a lot of ribbing for that third moniker), "Pop" to me, loved people and plants in that order and they loved him. Whether bowling for the St. Louis Cricket Club or judging a flower show, he did it with dash and humor.

He was born in 1885 in Exmouth, Devonshire, England and during early childhood moved with his family to Twickenham where he received his schooling. "When a young lad," he would tell me, "I helped clean flower pots at the famous Kew Gardens, walking a long distance each day to earn a few pence." Picture my surprise when as a teenager he first took me to see his English home and I found that "long" walk was just across a small green.

"Guess my legs were shorter then," he laughed.

Washing pots led to a romance with horticulture. "I wanted to be a student in the Queen's School of the Royal Botanic Garden at Kew, but they required one to be twenty-one years of age. So I decided to prepare myself by surreptitiously taking their written exams in physics, chemistry, etc., for practice. Boy, was I scared one day when the director called me into his office. I thought he would bounce me, instead he told me I'd done so well they had decided to set aside the age requirement for me."

"Young George" as he was called became the youngest student to train at Kew and when he graduated at twenty, the director offered him a job in Calcutta or St. Louis. "I think you'd make a better American with your brashness than an Indian," he was told.

A Career Blossoms

In 1906, when he arrived in St. Louis to be the foreman in charge of orchids and exotic plants at the Missouri Botanical Garden, he was asked what he thought of their orchid collection. "Well," he responded, 'you haven't much of one have you?"

On a boat trip to England, he met stunning Belle McAdie from Long Island. They married in 1910 and raised a family of four, George, Charles, Bradford (all of whom became horticulturists), and me (I married a botanist). Pop's wonderful world of flowers enfolded all of us.

He proceeded to build the three hundred orchid plants he found at Missouri into a world-famous collection of over fifty thousand specimens. To accomplished this, he went on numerous collecting trips to the jungles of Colombia and Panama.

Pop's contacts and foresight stimulated the establishment of MBG's tropical station in the Canal Zone for research in orchids and tropical plants. He became a charter member, trustee, and vice-president of the American Orchid Society, and organized as General Chairman the 1st World Orchid Conference, held in St. Louis in 1954.

Enter Water Lilies

Although he began his career as an orchid specialist, in 1912 his attention turned to breeding water lilies as well, "because I can see the results in a year rather than seven with orchids." Tropical water lilies became his great passion.

He introduced the day-blooming Whitaker Strain from Africa, for which he received the National Gardeners Association Gold Medal in 1920. His all-time favorite, which he hybridized in 1922 and named "Mrs. George H. Pring', was the first white hybrid day-blooming water lily. Other hybrids including the pink 'General Pershing' brought more awards in 1922 and 1923. One of his greatest introductions was the Lost Yellow Lily from Africa. He crossed it with 'Mrs. George H. Pring' and brought forth the famed 'St. Louis' in 1932, the first water lily of Garden creation granted a U.S. patent.

Walking home from elementary school each day through the Garden (we lived on the property), I often found Pop in hip boots, bent over in the middle of a lily pool pollinating the water lilies. "I'm going to name one for you someday," he told me, and 'Isabelle Pring', a viviparous white was the result. Imagine the thrill for a young-

77

ster to be so immortalized. Later, he produced a yellow one, 'Aviator Pring', named for my brother, Bradford, who had been killed in an army aircrash. Home gardeners rejoiced when he developed a pygmy water lily tiny enough to grow in a barrel. This he called 'Joanne Pring' after his first granddaughter.

He was appointed superintendent at MBG in 1928 and remained there until 1969—sixty-three years of joyous, devoted service. St. Louis knew him as "Mr. Answer Man" for he was never stumped with any question on plants. Over eight thousand requests a year came to his office and he was the first to respond to poison plant emergencies.

His last accomplishment of note in the field designing the magnificent lily pools at Longwood Gardens, Kennett Square, Pennsylvania. He spent his declining years there with my husband, Russell J. Seibert, and me. Although his eyesight failed, Pop recognized every plant by touch when taken through the conservatory. That was the mark of a true plant lover. ❀

SOURCES

There is now a new plant society devoted to sharing information on aquatic plants. Individuals interesting in joining should write to the Water-Lily Society, P.O. Box 104, Lilypons, Maryland 21717.

Kester's Wild Game Food Nurseries, Inc.
P.O. Box U
Omro, Wisconsin 54963

Lilypons Water Gardens
1500 Amhort Road
P.O. Box 10
Lilypons, Maryland 21717-0010

Paradise Gardens
16 May Street
Whitman, Massachusetts 02382

Scherer and Sons
104 Waterside Avenue
Northport, New York 11768

Slocum Water Gardens
1101 Cypress Garden Road
Winter Haven, Florida 33880

Superior Tropical Trading Co.
121 West Avenue
Hicksville, New York 11801

Waterford Gardens.
74 Allendale Avenue
P.O. Box 398
Saddle River, N.J. 07458

Van Ness Water Gardens
2460 North Euclid Avenue
Upland, California 91786

FURTHER READING

A GUIDE TO WATER GARDENING
by Philip Swindells, Scribners, New York.
1975

A MANUAL OF AQUATIC PLANTS
by Norman C. Fassett, University of
Wisconsin Press, Madison. 1957

**AQUATIC VASCULAR PLANTS OF
NEW ENGLAND:**
Part 1-7, by C.B. Hellquist and G.E. Crow.
New Hampshire Agricultural Experiment
Station, University of New Hampshire,
Durham, New Hampshire.

**COMMON MARSH, UNDERWATER
AND FLOATING-LEAVED PLANTS OF
THE U.S. & CANADA**
by Neil Hotchkiss. Dover Publications,
Inc., N.Y.

**EARTH PONDS—THE COUNTRY POND
MAKER'S GUIDE**
by Tim Matson. Countryman Press,
Woodstock, Vermont.

HOW TO KNOW THE AQUATIC PLANTS
by G.W. Prescott. Wm. C. Brown Company
Publishers, Dubuque, Iowa. 1969

ROCK AND WATER GARDENS
by Editors of Time-Life, Time-Life
Publishers, Alexandria, Va.

**THE COMPLETE GUIDE TO WATER
PLANTS**
by Helmut Muhlberg, Sterling Publishing
Co., Inc., N.Y.

THE DAMP GARDEN
by Beth Chatto. Biblio Distribution Center,
Totowa, N.J.

THE WATER GARDEN
by Frances Perry. Van Nostrand Reinhold,
New York.

WATER GARDENER'S HANDBOOK
by Philip Swindells. The Overlook Press.
N.Y.

WATER GARDENS
by Gordon T. Ledbetter. Interbook Inc.,
San Leandro, California.

Nymphaea *'Emily Grant Hutchings'*